McVICAR by himself

McVICAR

by himself

John McVicar

Artnik
Liechenstein

With thanks to: Peter Nash, Roy Hall, Tony Dunford
and Julian Broadhead.

First published in 1974.
This new and revised edition published
in Great Britain 2002, 3rd edition 2004.
Artnik Publishing
Landstrasse, 99
9494, Schaan, Liechenstein.
London Office:
341b Queenstown Road
SW8X 4LH, UK.

ISBN 1-903906-05-9

Printed in Spain by Cayfosa-Quebecor

CONTENTS

PART ONE: ESCAPE

PART TWO: MITIGATION PLEA

In memory of my mother, Diane.
For my wife forever, Valya.

PART ONE:

ESCAPE

JOHN McVICAR

Foreword

The first edition of this book was published in 1974 when John McVicar was serving 26 years for armed robbery and escaping from custody. He was paroled in 1978 and the following year Arrow Books published a paperback edition, which was aimed at exploiting the forthcoming release of the film *McVicar* (1980).

For reasons that we will come to, both of the earlier editions were inaccurate. When Artnik decided in 2002 to publish a new edition in which these earlier mistakes were corrected, McVicar had to ask Arrow to relinquish the rights to the book.

Despite the fact that the book had been out of print for twenty years, a then Arrow editor called Andy McPillock seemed to resent Artnik's intention to publish an accurate text. They made us wait 6 months before transferring the publishing rights. Thankfully, it proved worth waiting for as the book turned out to be a best-seller.

McVicar was surprised not merely by Artnik's request to re-print the book but also by its subsequent popularity. After all, the events it describes happened over 30 years ago! Yet, as far as we were concerned, the book was a classic that should never have gone out of print. It is up there with *Birdman of Alcatraz* and *Darkness at Noon*, even the prison book that most influenced McVicar – Oscar Wilde's *De Profundis*. He would vehemently disagree with these comparisons but one measure of the quality of *McVicar by himself* is that it inspired two films: *McVicar* and *The Shawshank Redemption.*

The main body of *McVicar by himself* is 'Escape' which tells the story of the two years that McVicar spent in HMP Durham's Special Wing. His presence there ended abruptly and, for the authorities, prematurely, when he escaped in October 1968. The escape story is racy, dramatic and very, very funny. It doesn't date because, as McVicar notes, "the prison system hardly changes".

It is also painfully realistic in that it shows what certain types of prisoners and prisons are really like. McVicar takes the reader inside – the real inside of prisons and prisoners. Yet, however ghastly, dreadful, and, in some cases, evil the prisoners are, they are never stripped of their humanity. The reader can even feel for a man like John Straffen, who throttled three young children, because McVicar describes him as he really was and, probably, still is after 52 years in prison.

As a writer McVicar is merciless in his commitment to realism but what always turns that into an enjoyable rather than a gruelling read is his humour. It is his eye for what is funny that makes this book a classic. There are also strains in the narrative that show a criminal who changed himself not through punishment, deterrence, rehabilitation, education, vocational training, romantic love, religion...but choice. The second part of *McVicar by himself* describes how he turned his own cold eye on himself and used what that revealed to change his character.

McVicar wrote 'Escape' after he was recaptured and was awaiting sentence on a number of charges relating to armed robbery and possession of firearms. He knew that the story had commercial potential. Part of his motive for writing it was to build up a nest egg for the woman with whom he'd been living with and their 7-year-old son.

The woman, Sheila W--------, had never worked except as a hostess in phoney drinking dens in the West End of London where punters were duped into buying expensive drinks on the promise of sex. Both parents protected the child from what were hardly the sort of parental careers that a boy would want to boast about to his school friends. However, with McVicar's arrest and certain exclusion from his son's life for at least the next ten years, the boy's future hardly looked promising. The woman, sadly, squandered the nest egg that McVicar left her and, since she never moved from the East End, the boy grew up in a similar environment to that of his father with predictable consequences.

However, when he wrote 'Escape', McVicar was also looking ahead to what he would do when he was released. He had already decided while he was on the run that if he were recaptured he would not try to escape or turn to crime when he was released. He said: "That was my own private deal with myself. And when recapture happened I never welshed on the deal by weaselling up fantasies that if my sentence became interminable I would think again about doing a runner." He faced the problem of what he would do when he was released and viewed 'Escape' as his first step to becoming a writer. He became completely absorbed in practising the skills of the trade and scribbled away almost compulsively.

Writing, then, became more than a means to cash in on his notoriety, but also a way of serving his time and preparing for a career. He started doing this within a few days of capture. *McVicar by himself* was published in 1974 and this edition coincides with the book's 30-year anniversary. He studied, too, passing exams and obtaining a degree and going onto a post-graduate thesis, constantly seeking to improve his chances of working as a writer once he was released.

But the way 'Escape' reached the outside had its own escape story to tell. After he was captured McVicar was imprisoned in HMP Brixton's special wing, where he completed the handwritten manuscript. He was locked up in a cell for 23 hours a day – the other hour was spent walking around the prison yard – and he wrote up the escape story on prison notepaper in tiny handwriting, using a makeshift table top as a desk. Prison rules explicitly forbid prisoners from writing memoirs for publication and since he was monitored like he was some kind of criminal Houdini he could not hide or disguise what he was doing. To cover up the purpose of writing, he told warders that he was working on his defence for the impending firearms' charges.

The warders never explicitly checked this and he was left to write his growing manuscript without interference. But he still had to smuggle it out. His visits were closed, although he did see his lawyers in open conditions. One of them agreed to take out his manuscript as long as the envelopes had 'defence documents' emblazoned on them. McVicar would then hand over his notes to the solicitor as if they were instructions on how his defence should be handled. The solicitor was never paid and acted out of nothing but good will. McVicar doesn't know whether he did it because he believed in his client's good intentions and saw it as his social duty to help a criminal who had turned over a new leaf or whether it was just a bit of corner cutting. Whatever, he remembers him as "one of the good guys in my life".

Once it was on the outside, the story still had to find a publisher! Eventually it landed up in the hands of a writer named Goronwy Rees. Rees was an establishment maverick. He was born in 1909, obtaining an Oxford scholarship at 21 – when he published his first novel – where he was friendly with Guy Burgess, Kim Philby, Anthony Blunt and the other Marxist fellow travellers; he became a distinguished social critic and writer, writing for The *Spectator, The Guardian* and *Encounter.* Twenty years after he died, evidence emerged that for three years prior to WW2 he had been on the KGB payroll.

McVicar was extremely lucky to find such a thoughtful and perceptive writer to edit his story but, as he never met or corresponded with him, Rees inevitably misinterpreted the handwritten prison scribblings. McVicar's handwriting is cramped and difficult to read at the best of times, but as he found it difficult to obtain the quantities of paper that he needed to do the job he reduced his prose to nigh on the limits of legibility. Rees necessarily had to interpret a lot of passages. Nonetheless, he did transcribe a handwritten 50,000 words, publish them and obtain serialisation in the *Sunday Times*!

Roger Daltrey who was then the lead singer in the rock band The Who actually read the extracts in the *Sunday Times* and became intrigued with playing McVicar in a film. Later he bought the film rights of *McVicar by himself* for the princely sum of £2,000. Luckily for

McVicar, Bill Curbishley, manager of The Who, locked up the money in a solicitor's account where nobody but its owner could access it. It was to be the only money McVicar had when he was released in 1978.

Curbishley had served time, so he knew a bit about how a prisoner's money can disappear into the pockets of needy relations or girlfriends. He had been sentenced to 12 years for armed robbery in the 60s and early 70s. Unlike McVicar's convictions, Curbishley's was a grotesque miscarriage of justice as he had nothing to do with the robbery and didn't even know the actual culprits. The evidence on which Curbishley and another man, Bill Stubbles, were convicted was fabricated but their convictions have never been overturned.

Eventually, the film went into pre-production with a playwright named Alan Clarke writing the script. He soon had enough of Daltrey directing what he was writing, and left the project. McVicar was asked to try his hand. After Daltrey rejected his first film script on the grounds that it didn't contain enough romance with the female lead, Cheryl Campbell, McVicar came up with one that secured Daltrey's approval.

When the film went into production, McVicar left Leicester University, where he was doing an M.phil., for London and Pinewood Studios. A lot of the *McVicar* script was written while the film was being shot.

McVicar tends to be quite cynical about the film: "Daltrey wanted a part that gave him the opportunity to show himself as a great actor in a romantic lead. How he could do that playing the life of a failed East London robber who, while he was on the run, hooked up with a deadbeat clip-joint hostess defeats me, but it probably explains why afterwards I was never commissioned to write another film script and Daltrey never got another lead part." Nonetheless, the film was phenomenally successful and over twenty years after it went on release, the video is still selling...if only just.

Stephen King's *Shawshank Redemption* copied the same tunnelling out method of escape from prison that was used in *McVicar*, but he also used the premise that a person can lead a proper life in prison. Moreover, in making the choices necessary to lead a proper life, the convict can redeem himself, can make himself a better person. This process has nothing to do with reform or rehabilitation; indeed McVicar, like his idol Oscar Wilde, has utter contempt for those people who try to reform or rehabilitate criminals.

The Shawshank Redemption is one of the most popular films of the 20th century. It strikes such a popular chord because, despite being set in prison, it is true to life. People in a difficult environment are depicted as making moral choices that add to or detract from their character. It is a million miles away from the reductive take on the human condition of what McVicar calls the "prisoner-reform industry".

Ironically, one of the consequences of his contempt for this industry is that he has become unpopular with the many journalists who are sympathetic to its cause. A web-search of his name will bring up hundreds of references to him that almost invariably tag him with his criminal past.

Despite the fact that his last crime was over 30 years ago, journalists consistently use such descriptions as "ex-convict" and "ex-armed robber" or "armed robber turned author" but never date when he was in prison or a criminal. The impression is thereby created that he only recently gave up crime and turned to writing.

Yet, on the rare occasion when they do date his criminal past, they find other ways to let it overshadow what he has been doing for the last 25 years. When his book on the murder of Jill Dando was published (*Dead on Time*, 2002, Blake), he was persuaded much against his own better judgement by John Blake to give an interview to the *Telegraph Magazine*. His position was "the Telegraph always do me and they aren't going to stop because of this book".

The Telegraph did do him…in spades. They got the photographer to take black and white head shots that stylistically were like stock mugshots of a criminal. The interviewer, a woman called Mitchison, even dredged up some real mugshots of McVicar from the 60s to illustrate her piece and deliberately used Rees' version of McVicar by himself even though she was told it was inaccurate and was sent a modern version.

McVicar read the opening of the article, took in the mugshots, then immediately tossed the magazine aside, saying, "I knew this guttersnipe was going to do me and she has. I author a book on why Barry George executed Jill Dando and this unread nobody focuses on what I was doing 40 years ago!" He spent the next half an hour blaming everyone but himself for giving the interview.

His wife Valentina commented more thoughtfully on this kind of journalism: "It is singularly mean-spirited to define people by the lowest point in their life and in doing so dismiss a long writing career."

It is not all one-way traffic, though, with the *Telegraph*. Artnik's office is decorated with one framed email that McVicar sent to another *Telegraph* journalist: "You're a liar. I am sick and tired of lowlife journos like you cooking up copy about us. At the moment, I am up to my neck in work and I don't have time other than to write this. But If I see you out on the stump I will clump you around the ear, and you can put that in your column and smoke it." The columnist neither replied nor did he print the email.

In 2002, McVicar married the founder of Artnik, Valentina Artsrunik, and they live together between their homes on the Black Sea and London. He now works as an editor for the publishing house.

ARTNIK, February 2004.

Chapter 1
Getting to the hell-hole

Durham is the worst prison in Britain...well, in 1968, that was the way us twenty cons in its long-term wing had it. I doubt if the 1400 or so short-termers in the main prison would have disagreed with us but, as we were isolated in E-Wing, we didn't know or, for that matter, care.

Charlie Richardson went further and described E-Wing as "the hell-hole" and the name kind of stuck. Except for Charlie, we all used the term tongue in cheek because it would wind up the screws in the wing, who were in a continual state of outrage over how easy we had it. Charlie, though, was one of those people who got whipped up by his own propaganda and when he was running down Durham, E-Wing and especially the Geordie screws keeping us there, he sounded like some redneck Baptist preacher rounding on his flock. As a rule, no convict likes his jail and the longer he is serving the greater his dislike, but even allowing that Charlie was on 25 years he was hardly suffering eternal damnation in Dante's *Inferno*.

Aside from what we or Charlie thought, most of the inhabitants of Durham Town, with its old cathedral and university, regarded HMP Durham as an abomination – but they have always had to suffer something for the privilege of living and prospering within their naturally fortified boundaries. In days of old, Durham was regarded as fair and rich game for the reivers on their sorties after cattle, and these rustlers were regarded as connoisseurs in such matters.

In the 1960s, the only cattle left in Durham Town were the prisoners and they were farmed by the screws. Tradition was not entirely lost though, since those Durham screws had a little of the reivers' steely blood coursing through their veins. They like their meat red and raw and their favourite cut was a piece of London convict.

In the late fifties, when the Prison Department decided it needed a special unit for prison nuisances – which London produced in abundance – Durham was its natural choice. A small unit inside Durham Prison, called E-Wing, became the country's punishment wing and the treatment provided for the rebellious, the recalcitrant and the incorrigible of the penal system was the time-honoured one of a good kicking.

It worked a treat: other governors sitting behind their big desks found the job that much easier for the unit being there to do their dirty work. Eventually the place was closed down and an enquiry set up to exonerate the staff from the malicious accusations made against them by their unwilling guests. But like all good things, you can't keep a hard nick down and, in 1965, up sprung E-Wing in a new guise – as a Special Wing for a new breed of London con. These were the Super Crooks of the 1960s – the Great Train Robbers. Durham's Chief Constable at the time got the locals in a lather when he issued the following statement about one of them, Gordon Goody, who had been sentenced to 30 years for his part in the 1961

£2.6 million heist:

"I am satisfied that Goody's friends were prepared to launch something in the nature of a full scale military attack, even to the extent of using tanks, bombs and what the army describes as limited atomic weapons... A couple of tanks could easily come through the streets of Durham unchallenged. Nothing is too extravagant." Quite. The Chief Constable's press release hardly raised confidence among the people of Durham that the prison was an asset to the town.

E-Wing had received a full scale security face-lift: CCTVs covered the whole of the wing; electronic locking fitted to all the wing's entrances; monitoring warders sat in bullet-proof glass cubicles; razor-wire necklaced anything remotely scaleable; guard dogs patrolled...but old habits die hard. The Prison Department forgot to tell the screws that E-Wing was no longer for punishment but for security. Goody took to asking for his dog-collar but some of the other members of the gang were of a less hardy disposition and wilted under the harassment and goading. Questions were asked in the House of Commons. Gradually conditions eased.

******

Meanwhile, for over four years, I had been doing my thing and, in recognition of all the employment my activities were creating for security guards, police officers, court officials and judges, I was awarded the exemplary sentence of twenty-three years. When it was passed it not only seemed impossible to serve, but I had no intention of even trying. Plotting to escape is one way of serving your sentence that excuses you from having to wait until it's finished. Such a course, though, is not without its risks.

I had started off with 8 years in 1965, then in 1966 escaped from Parkhurst Prison, went back at it for the five months I was at liberty. On re-capture, I was sentenced to 15 years "to run consecutive with the 8 years you are already serving, making 23 years in all". Justice Hinchcliffe was renowned for doing a prisoner's arithmetic for him – after abolition, judges like Hinchcliffe at least kept the spirit of capital punishment alive.

I spent a year in the punishment cells at Wandsworth before being swagged from the Old Bailey in early September 1967 to Chelmsford Prison. I had been tried for some other robbery and found guilty but the judge just gave me five years concurrent. Who cared? I was rather more pleased with my escort: motorbike outriders punching holes through the traffic, squad cars back and front, helicopter overhead. I mean if I'd been in a fat, old Roller surrounded by flunkeys instead of turnkeys I might have languidly waved my hand at the gawping onlookers. The trouble was my handcuffs prevented me but, all the same, the attention did make me feel at least as important as a Royal Mail Great Train robber.

Naturally, at moments like this, I was aware that despite all the attention and the gratifying drain that I was having on the public purse that night I would be put in another kennel and would not be ordering three grams of uncut coke from my dealer, recruiting a couple of hookers from Tramp and, while I was waiting for them to arrive, opening a couple of bottles of Krug. Nevertheless, while I waited for the natural order to re-assert itself, I did try to look on the bright side of life and kept my eyes open for an escape hatch.

Chelmsford Prison had its own security wing, which was really an Essex version of what they had up in Durham. It was a cheapskate job with none of the electronic toys or gadgets that were standard in the other wings; instead Chelmsford had a funny little Governor called Captain Davies who wore his regiment's tie under a Hitlerite moustache. The warders saluted him when he made an entrance. Thankfully, his brisk military gait meant he was never around for very long, but what little contact we had was enough for us both to know we were on opposite sides of the trenches.

I knew that I would not be staying in Chelmsford. It wasn't good for my dignity being in a Special Wing that didn't meet modern spec but, at the same time, that meant loopholes. And was there one in Captain's Davies' joint... Right up on the top landing in the ceiling of the ablutions' recess there was a trap door that led out onto the roof. It was secured by this little itsy-bitsy padlock that even if you were playing bondage games you would have balked at using to secure your lady to the bed. It became a shrine to me. During association, while others were playing table tennis and watching TV, I used to climb the stairs to the top landing and go along to the recess then look up at the trapdoor and its securing padlock in awe. It was my magic carpet to crime, coke, hookers and Krug.

I had to recruit a bunch of wannabe escapees, which in Chelmsford's Security Wing was not easy. Most of the cons were too flattered at being deemed a security risk to want to escape. After a month, though, nine of us went to work. We bundled the screws on alarm posts into nearby cells, then went through the trapdoor but, as we did, someone on the bottom landing knocked over a table load of cups. Probably excitement. It blew the whistle on us as a warder in the adjoining wing looked in and saw no staff manning the alarm posts.

However, we were already smashing through the roof tiles, then with a sheet-rope slithering down onto the prison grounds. As the scream went up with sirens and whistles and floodlights, we grouped at the bottom of the wall that was between us and two stolen cars parked a couple of streets away. It was a good moment. There was just the formality of throwing up the sheet-rope with its attached hook onto the top of the wall, then climbing up and dropping down to freedom and robbing banks. Obviously serving the longest sentence and, with all my physical training, the honours fell to me.

I had about three tries and each time it fell short. Everybody started to look apprehensive; here we were out of the security wing, against the outside wall, without a screw in sight, with a rope and a hook and I couldn't do the easy bit. Aside from the disappointment it was very embarrassing for me. I had another five or so tries, then in disgrace I yielded to popular demand that someone else had a go. But they got no more joy than me. The trouble was my responsibility went further than not being able to chuck it up – I had supervised the guy who'd constructed the hook part and despite his objections I'd insisted that he should weight it according to my specifications. Fortunately, he only made the hook, and didn't participate in the break-out, otherwise he'd have probably put the rope around my neck.

Someone shouted, "Screws!" I saw four of them standing about twenty yards away, watching us. We were shy of audiences and ran around the nick next to the wall, hoping to find a lower section. By now all the cons in the main prison were at their windows shouting encouragement to us as we came into sight. The joint was jumping. It didn't help us, because our next three or four attempts to snag the top of the wall were, if anything, even less successful. Finally, still avoiding the pursuing screws, we arrived at the front gate, where Captain Davies received us with another squad of his men. There were about a dozen in all.

It's bad enough losing when you think you've won, but it's far worse to lose when you know you should have won. I'd fouled up a winning hand. A few moments ago, standing at the wall, I'd thought that throwing the hook was merely the prelude to going home, a formality. Now I was facing the punishment cells nursing the pains of a good kicking. The ignominy of it! I remembered when I was about twenty being released from some disgusting prison and going out that night on the prowl and being picked up by some luscious thing who thought my two years' sexual abstinence would make her night. It didn't work out like that. Instead of it being a rod of iron it was a rag doll. I knew the Chelsmford debacle was pasted forever in my scrapbook of cringe-at-the-memories.

A most un-military Captain Davies was now flapping about like a turkey who had found out about Christmas. He said, "It's no good, lads. The place is surrounded by troops. Come in quickly and don't let's have any trouble."

A few of the screws were holding riot sticks and one of my escapee recruits, Martin O'Day, pointed at one of them, and screamed at Davies: "No trouble! What's he got a riot stick for then? You're going to cosh us up." I used to wonder sometimes at Martin's capacity for surprise. What did he think they were going to do? Tell us a bedtime story!

The screw hid the stick behind his back, looking sheepish – which probably endeared him to Captain Davies who is after all Welsh.

"Come on, lads," said Captain Davies. "It was a good try."

We all ignored him as did his screws, as well. They wanted an order to get stuck in, not listen to Davies trying to sweet-talk us. We were milling around feeling sick. Freddie Sampson said to no one in particular, "I can't believe it. I just can't believe it. I was sure we'd made it." He was staring at the ground shaking his head in disbelief. I remembered once playing football against Freddie, who was useful on the ball, but I'd dispossessed him and was moving off to set up a play when he killed my pass with a tug on the shirt. He was cunning, too – did it on the blind side of the ref. This memory blocked me from empathising with Freddie at the moment. Thoughts like this go through your mind even when someone has confiscated the Krug just as you were about to drink.

Captain Davies was really in a bad way – he turned to me for help. "McVicar, lad, come in," he wheedled. "It was a good try but it's over. You might as well come in now." When I told him that *they* – meaning the others – didn't want to come in, he continued hopefully, "Maybe not, but they will if you go in." I was the leader of the gang again…the leader who couldn't snag the hook on the top of the wall.

Martin was still holding the hook while Teddy, a swarthy little gypsy, had hold of the end of the attached sheet-rope. He made a loop out of it, and came up behind Davies, who was still trying to persuade me to do his bidding. Teddy said to Davies: "I am going to hang you, you Welsh mountain goat. This is all your fucking fault."

Of course, it was all his fault. If his nick had been a bit more hospitable, then we would not have wanted to escape. And when we did decide to try, there was this open invitation in that flimsy padlock securing a trapdoor that led onto the roof. Complete shambles; utterly irresponsible.

I was walking slowly along, sunk in gloom. Captain Davies, still looking warily at Teddy, was in a daze but still talking to me. He had started walking around me to keep away from Teddy who was following him holding the noosed rope. Martin, who was holding the hook attached to the rope, now trailed Teddy. They were circling me as I walked along still trying to come to terms with the ignominy of it all. Davies was chuntering away, "You might as well give yourselves up. We can forget this ever happened... There doesn't have to be any loss of remission as long as we resolve matters sensibly. Come in and I will give the order to the troops to return to the barracks."

He was barking, of course. The strain of losing some over the wall: Home Office inquiries, reports to fill out, press briefings...demotion to an open prison... no more security wings. It was understandable.

The ludicrousness of it all got to me. It is only by seeing the farce in tragedy that you can keep up the obduracy to repeat it. I decided to show a bit of leadership. "Let's go back the way we came out," I suggested to the others. This got the nod from those who had recovered sufficiently to vote. We walked round to the point where we had originally dropped down. Davies had given up trying to grovel to me and was now at the head of a swathe of warders, some openly swinging their riot sticks. Although he recovered some of his dignity and military bearing, Davies was still incapable of taking command.

A few of my mob started to talk about making a demonstration on top of the roof. Davies relapsed as everyone started to climb back to the top of the wing. His expression showed his panic as the image of us cavorting around on the roof replaced that of us haring through the streets of Chelsmford. He came up close to us; there was just Fred and me on the ground. "Go on, John," Fred said. Fred's as game as a bagel, but as he had about as much meat on him as a butcher's pencil he was hardly built for a rugby scrum with Davies' heavy mob. In fact, his diminutive size is probably why he became a shameless shirt-tugger on the football field.

"No," I said. "I'm on 23, you're outranked." He was only doing twelve years. I bunked him up the first bit. He started the long climb up the dangling sheet-rope to the roof. I watched him go, waiting to see if Davies would have the nerve to grab me or at least order his men to. I was unarmed and on my own. He had about twenty warders around him, all watching the stand-off between us. I eyeballed him insolently. I could see the indecision on his face – he knew what he should do but he couldn't do it. He was just staring into the headlights. When Fred made it, I grabbed the bottom and began hauling myself up. Davies stood next to me watching me go.

If he is still alive, I know the memory still makes the sweat pop out of his forehead. He'll never forget it...some memories only death deletes. Afterwards one warder who watched it said to me, "He should never have let you go up on that roof." Which was the understatement of the year in view of what I got up to when I was there.

A few of my mob were so sick they couldn't whip up any enthusiasm for a demonstration, but four of us pulled ourselves together and had a splendid time pulling slates off, smashing the roof timbers and tearing the tarpaulin underneath. We were all scampering around like mischievous chimps on the forest's canopy. *Destroying prison property.* Just the phrase – it is actually a disciplinary charge – is enough to warm the cockles of any ex-con's heart. What a lovely way to spend the day.

The next discovery was the delights of slate throwing. Martin O'Day quickly discovered that he was a natural at mastering the aerodynamic properties of a skimming slate. It was like bouncing stones on the waves, except we were thirty feet up, the slates were about a foot square, weighed in at just under a pound and we had all manner of inviting targets to aim at. Below us, on the exercise yards, there were clusters of screws, police, firemen and sundry men in suits standing around looking up at us. Over the prison wall, a hundred or so rubberneckers had gathered to watch the action. Martin quickly found his mark and soon had everyone on the ground running around like headless chickens.

The slates zipped through the air like stone axeheads and when they hit the ground or a wall they shattered like a gunshot ricochet. We had an arsenal of flying guillotines. Some of the screws took it upon themselves to play chicken and dodge the missiles as they rained down. But it was a dangerous game and most just scattered and ran for cover. The next minute riot shields were issued and a centurion guard inched its way out onto the yard with Captain Davies sheltered in the middle holding a megaphone.

"This is the Governor speaking. This is an order – you are to come down and surrender..." This was greeted with a volley of abuse from the artillery on the rooftop. There were the familiar comments that one hears in such circumstances: "Wanker...Cunt...Fuck off." While Martin was organising the slate-throwing corps to mount a concerted attack on the shielded carapace protecting Captain Davies, I turned to Fred and said excitedly, "This beats escaping, doesn't it?"

He gave me a long withering look before saying bluntly, "No it doesn't."

Davies was still blathering away: "...I must warn you, this is mutiny. If you do not surrender immediately, I shall be ordering the Fire Service to hose you down. This is your last chance – That is an order." So it went on. However, Martin's fusillade suddenly broke the overlapping shields of the carapace. One screw went down and two others broke ranks to help him. The rest scuttled off like ants under the boiling water. Davies dropped his megaphone and ran too. We all broke into a victory cheer, the crowd outside who couldn't see what we were celebrating cheered back. But we had obviously gone one up on the prison staff.

Next came some spotlights on us, then a couple of fire engines drove onto the yard and out came the hoses. We got a bit worked up at the sight of the hoses being uncoiled and we set up a barrage of skimming tiles. It certainly kept them on their toes but the firemen were made of sterner stuff than the screws and they kept to their task. With the roof lit up like a floodlit pitch, some policemen began taking photographs of us...presumably for evidence. Then, some press photographers also joined in from outside the wall. They must have been about thirty yards away from us.

Two hoses began to splutter into life. The parabolas of water built up and got their range. We all stopped throwing slates and held on for dear life to the exposed timber struts. It was a long way down if you were washed off the roof. Thoughts of falling and breaking my back began to terrify me. With some people it is cockroaches, others heights... My worst nightmare is the paraplegic one. It is a lot worse being quadriplegic but my room 101 is paralysis from the waist down. The rag doll: to never be able to get it up but remembering when you could. I was clinging to my bit of timber like Geoffrey Boycott did his wicket. I was soaked but I wasn't sure if some of it was a voided bladder.

However, the water pressure was pretty tame. Obviously, the aim was to make us uncomfortable not to dislodge us. Once we realised this we recovered our swagger and braggadocio. Martin was first on his feet opening his arms to the water. "I can piss better than that," he shouted. Martin was not one of those men who clears the shower when he enters but I am sure if he had been he would have proceeded to demonstrate.

We began targeting the fireman. Occasionally we'd score a hit and they'd scatter but gradually everyone lost interest, including us. Once they left us alone and we had no targets to aim at, the rooftop was not so homely. The audience dispersed, too. With no one paying attention to us, the situation began to pall. It was cold and we were still wet. We began to drift in through the trapdoor where the reception committee was waiting to receive us and read the riot act. Someone had negotiated that magistrates should be on hand to witness the surrender, so we would be spared a kicking. I came in last but before I did I took the iron hook off the clambering rope and went on the rampage smashing the whole of the wing's roof to smithereens. It kept me warm and raised the price of incarcerating me.

It was about three o'clock in morning when I clambered down through the trapdoor into the recess. Captain Davies stood there with a few screws and a bored magistrate. I washed my tarred hands in a washbasin. No one said anything. Davies watched me like I'd crawled out from under the rock he was going to crush me with. The exhibition that he'd made of himself earlier was out of mind but still filed away in the long-term memory where it would pop out on the odd occasion to spoil a good night's sleep.

In my cell that night, I tried to come to terms with how I had bungled the only chance of escape I might well get – the rooftop protest had really been a way of putting off the reckoning. Now that kicked in with a vengeance. As in life generally, when you miss a high tide you can sink into the sand and never live to float on another one. I knew that I might never get another chance like the one I'd just squandered. It was a troubling night that stole more than sleep.

Eventually, I and my fellow freedom-lovers appeared before a visiting magistrates' board (the body that adjudicates all serious disciplinary offences) to face all sorts of charges in connection with the botched escape. These hearings were heard in an office on the bottom landing of our wing; occasionally I'd seen cons from the main prison waiting outside for adjudication. They would be shaved, polished, pressed and on best parade ground behaviour. Prison staff – like Davies – often have a military background and relish a prison that runs on the same good order, discipline and obedience found in the army. At its most basic they are all obsessed with addressing each other as "sir" and making us call them sir.

I hadn't addressed a screw as *sir* since I was at Reading Prison, when it was a punishment borstal where even a bit of dumb insolence would get the shit beaten out of you. In fact, the longer my sentence got, the better I became at subverting the spit-and-polish mentality. I discovered that walking about in your underpants – baggy, prison issue – worked rather well. Anyway, underpants became the dress order of the day when we appeared before the visiting magistrates. As I also had my hair cropped and a longer stubble on my face I did not look at all the sort of prisoner magistrates would want on their adjudication mat.

I sauntered into the office, which was packed with screws, and stood before three Chelmsford worthies who had Davies sitting next to them. Behind them was a young, rather dowdy secretary wearing an old-fashioned, swirly frock. The portly worthies all looked bewildered; Davies had his po-faced, this-is-nothing-to-do-with-me expression; the secretary just looked disgusted. In fact, it was so blatant, I had a quick peek down to see if anything was poking out of the underpants. I have my standards. Mad Frankie Fraser used to think nothing of appearing naked with his own excrement smeared over himself for these adjudication calls. I always thought this went beyond the call of duty of even a dedicated subversive.

The chairman – the one in the middle - treated me with the kind of tact and consideration that one normally reserves for the mentally retarded. He read out the charges and explained what rights I had in defending myself. I began grunting and mumbling like some feral child that had been discovered in an attic. The chairman looked more sorry for me than anything else and courteously repeated it all over again, enunciating every word very distinctly, lingering apologetically over the longer ones. "You may…if you wish to, contest the charges…hear the evidence against you and ask questions through me of any officer who gives evidence…"

As he spoke, Davies just stared stonily into space. I then had one of those out-of-body experiences when you are up above the room looking down on everyone including yourself. Suddenly it all seemed so pointless; what I was doing went to nothing. All the people in the room were paid to be there…except me. I had to be there because I had gambled my freedom for money and lost. I owed the State 23 years of prime lifetime. I had played poker with my life and lost my stake. Now all I could do was tip over the card table.

I decided I would rather be in my cell with a book. I replaced my gormless look with one of disdain and replied confidently, "That will be quite all right. I fully understand the charges and what rights I enjoy before this tribunal. I plead guilty to all charges and enter no mitigatory pleas in respect of punishment. Thank you." I stifled my proposed punch line, "Please do your worst." I'd gone civilised and it seemed proper to stay in character.

At least all the visitors including the disgusted secretary were nonplussed but suddenly I lost heart for staging these side-shows. While wasting everyone else's time I was also wasting my own. Okay, there wasn't much I could do with it, but I could write a letter, carry on reading *Troilus and Cressida*, even have a wank. Anything was better than playing the clown with people who were employed to let me do it. I knew I had to learn to lose and stop chasing my losses...but not just yet. As I watched the three magistrates confer briefly – for form's sake, as my punishment was predetermined, I remembered a line from the play: 'Those wounds heal ill that men do give themselves.' It said something about me that I was going to have to face...but also not just yet.

For a couple of months I kept my head down while I served out my punishment. I ignored Captain Davies when he came to my cell on his daily visit to those on punishment. However, when my punishment was over, I was put on Rule 43 because I was 'a threat to good order and discipline'. Next time Davies appeared, I tried to talk to him when he came to my cell door but he just looked at me contemptuously and took no notice. That put him one up on me. The next day when I went out on the exercise yard, I refused to come in after my time was up. Six screws gathered round me and there was the usual stand off. As they tried to persuade me, they kept inching closer, while I kept out of grabbing distance and threatened them whenever they got too near. We were all back in the playground.

Eventually the Chief Officer – the head screw is secondary to the governor but in many prisons they carry more clout – came out onto the yard. He ordered his men to take me in by force but I was moving around very quickly, which meant that the first one to grab me would be on his own and vulnerable until his mates piled in. This went on for about five minutes until he said, "Look Mac, you are going to come in either voluntarily or by force. If you won't come in under your own steam, I am going to call up extra staff and we will take you whatever you do. It's up to you."

As I am always one for reading the writing on the wall, especially when it is written in my blood, I relented. "Alright, chief," I said, "I'll come in now because out here I'm on a hiding to nothing, but if I'm not moved in three days, I'm going to smash a screw. I won't give him a chance, just as you're not giving me one."

I'm a great one for giving such ultimatums but not very good at carrying them out. I can't really whack someone until they have whacked me first. Even on the pavement, I always give guards the chance of handing over the prize peacefully and only shoot them if they refuse. I think it is to do with growing up on the playing fields of the East End. I was always engaged in some sport but whatever it was I religiously abided by the rules. I could no more have tugged a shirt on the football pitch than rob my own mother. In fact, I am sure that this fair play conditioning had a lot to do with my being so hopeless at crime.

However, two days later my cell was unlocked and I was told to pack my kit – I was being transferred. I got my odds and ends together, said goodbye to all my pals through their cell doors and went downstairs. Captain Davies was on parade with about fifteen screws in attendance. We walked out of the Special Wing to reception where I signed the private property book for the items I was arrested in. Davies was in the next room but before they handcuffed me I heard him say, "Make him wear a jacket." A few moments later a nice sort of screw came in holding a prison donkey jacket. He said apologetically, "Mac, put this on."

It was my turn now. "You're joking, ain't yer," I said. "Tell Captain Wanker to put it on himself." He went back to Davies, obviously to report the refusal. There were mutterings before four screws came back into the reception room with the same screw holding the same jacket. He said, "You've got to put it on or the governor's ordered us to make you."

Poor Davies – he had impeccable bad timing. Probably a five car escort was waiting to roll with full scale logistical back-up and he thought he could make me wear a jacket that would have had to have a gun secreted in the pocket for me to comply. I just grinned. Moments like this made it all worthwhile. "Has he? Well, surprise, surprise, I ain't putting it on." They started to walk towards me and I backed off into a corner and shaped up. I look the business when I shape up. The fists are half-clenched, slightly off-guard, but swaying like cobra heads; my head moves slightly and the eyes are right on for the opening to bomb the big right hand. If it went on looks you would think I could punch a hole in a cell door. It's definitely one of my best effects.

There was a bit more manoeuvring until one of them, a senior screw, took the disputed jacket from my putative dresser and carried it back to Davies. I heard him say, very emphatically, "He won't wear it, sir." I didn't hear Davies' reply, but it was a walkover. I was never going to lose this one. The next minute they handcuffed me to a senior screw, then with the escort in tow we walked out of reception and got into a police car that was ticking over outside the door. I was in the back seat with a screw either side of me. There was usual liaising by the driver via the radio with the vehicles outside.

Next to the car Davies and the chief screw were overseeing the assembly of the cavalcade – the car window between us was open. I asked the screw next to me, "Where we going – Durham or Parkhurst?" I knew he wouldn't tell but as he ummed and ahhed about not knowing himself, Davies couldn't resist it. He leaned over and snapped, "Broadmoor." In fact, we went to Durham.

In prison, though, even trifling victories can have a long-incubating sting in the tail. Two days after being recaptured, over three years after leaving Chelmsford, I had to speak to the deputy governor in Brixton about a visit. It was virtually around the time that I started to write this escape story. In the course of our conversation he casually remarked, "Oh, by the way, I was talking on the phone yesterday to an old friend of yours." I knew it could not be a friend but I hadn't a clue what was coming. I looked quizzically at him. "Captain Davies," he replied. "And he asked to be remembered to you."

Yes, he would like to remind me of the pleasure my recapture gave him. Yet, as I walked back to my cell to start writing again, I thought about Davies going to all that trouble. He should have been cooler and not played his get-back so soon.

But he couldn't...the memory still made him cringe.

Chapter 2
The hell-hole

Durham's E-Wing is an L-shaped block of cells, four stories high. The two gates leading into it are on the bottom landing at either end of the L. The cells on the bottom landing – the Ones – were largely for administration and the thirty or so prisoners located in the wing when I arrived were scattered around the top three landings – Twos, Threes and Fours. There were two sex cases held on protection on the second landing – Ian Brady, the Moors murderer, and David Burgess, who murdered two children. They were kept separate and isolated.

Any crime connected with sex makes a prisoner suspect but any tampering with children, especially sexual murder, turns him into a pariah. A sex case or "nonce" is viewed as worse than an informer or "grass" – even screws are held in higher esteem by mainstream cons than nonces or grasses. "Nick–sniffers" – liberals who take up prison reform – are always appalled and shocked by the way that normal prisoners reject and attack nonces. They appreciate why informers are rejected and can sympathise with such an attitude, but not nonces. The reason for this is they regard nonces as ill and not responsible for their actions, as needing treatment or counselling. Yet, most nonces are as responsible for their actions as the common car thief or burglar and derive no more benefit from treatment than do the latter.

Like much of the liberal's mindset, nick-sniffers are profoundly wrong about this. The test of whether a person is mentally ill or disturbed does not lie in his motive but in how he executes what he is motivated to do. Does he demonstrate that he was capable of not doing what he did? Is there a method in the gratification? In fact, as a rule, paedophiles exhibit more foresight and method in their crimes than car thieves or burglars. Nick-sniffers conflate motive with *modus operandi* and where they think the motive is sick they assume that the crime must be too. They are actually quite distinct.

****

There was no work in E–Wing and you either stayed in your cell or congregated in two rooms where you sat around chatting or listening to the radio. There was a tiny little exercise yard, which most of us didn't bother to use for our statutory hour every day. The cons were divided up into two groups for evening association, taking alternative evenings, when we could watch TV between 6 pm and 9 pm and train with the weightlifting equipment from six to seven-thirty. There were hot water urns for tea or instant coffee, which could be brought from the canteen, and an electric oven downstairs where one could make an evening snack such as baked beans on toast.

When I arrived, although I had finished my punishment for the Chelmsford rumpus, I had to do another month behind my door. I did what I always do on lock–down: have a workout in my cell every day, read books and, as long as I could secure a broadsheet newspaper like *The Times* or *The Guardian*, do the crossword. Well, half do it. I went onto normal routine just before Christmas 1967, grateful to be able to relax and exchange gossip with the other cons. It seemed that I had been on punishment for years and I wanted a breather from trouble.

I knew a few of the other cons. "Mad" Frankie Fraser was there, hopping around on a walking stick because of a beating he had received after the Parkhurst riot. As he often reminds people, he is not mad but, given that he has been certified twice for his one-man war with the prison system, the tag sticks. Anyway, as he once said, "I can hardly call myself Sane Frankie Fraser."

While he may be sane, he is still evil. The torturing that he did for the Richardson gang was as macabre as it gets. One of Frank's specialities was to mete out just deserts to the people who were periodically nailed under the floorboards in Charlie Richardson's scrap yard. Fraser would leave a nightclub where he would pick up a plate, knife and fork and some ketchup, then drive back to the yard with a couple of mates to unprise the prisoner. Then, he or one of his mates would excrete on the plate and on threat of electric shock torture the victim would be forced to eat it. Frank liked to provide a running commentary to the meal incorporating the man's offences: "You've been a fucking grass, haven't you. But we feed you. Just put plenty of ketchup on it and you'll enjoy it...That's it my son. Get it down you." As a further humiliation, for their dessert, Fraser would then sodomise his captives.

The Durham warder did not like Frank's walking stick as he was in the habit of brandishing it under their noses. One of them came up with the observation that as Frank was on a walking stick it was too dangerous for him to walk up and down the stairs linking the different landings. The doctor heartily agreed and, as Frank was grounded on the bottom landing, this meant he could not go up to any association room to watch TV. After much huffing and puffing he gave up his walking stick. Thankfully, he was transferred soon after I arrived. I had been friendly with one of the men he tortured, Peter Fallon and, whenever I saw Fraser, I always thought of what he did to him.

The two Richardson brothers were there and whenever I got down with my 23-year sentence I would look at Charlie's card on the docket outside his cell: "Sentence 25 years". His brother Eddie was serving 15 years. Otherwise all I did was hump the barbell up and down, look at TV and wait for something to happen. Something eventually would – it always does in prison – but I certainly had no intention of instigating it.

Changes were supposed to be coming to the wing. A proper exercise yard was being built, and an ironmongery workshop was also under construction. In February, a new prison governor, "Flash" Gordon, and a new assistant governor for the wing, Alan Greene, were appointed. Nothing changed and no one took much notice of them; but Gordon was noticing us and most of what he noticed he didn't like.

His first notable move was to invite Brady and Burgess out to watch TV. Brady had more sense than to accept, but Burgess was only a kid, nineteen, and naive enough to think he might find a friendly face. Burgess had raped and murdered two 9-year-old girls in a gravel pit – the father of one of the girls discovered his daughter's body. Burgess's crimes were as foul as they come. When I saw him going on exercise or just slopping out I used to feel that I owed the father some vengeance but I wasn't prepared to take on three screws to enact it.

When he came out to watch TV, I was lifting weights downstairs on the bottom landing. The word spread like wildfire that he was in the TV room on the third landing with a screw next to him. I didn't like it but I wasn't going to get burnt up about it. Someone would do something. But no one did.

After I'd showered, I walked upstairs to the TV room where he was sitting next to a screw by the door with perhaps 11 other cons in the same room. Just looking at the scumbag made my stomach knot up but I wasn't going to go over the top first. I thought the first thing was to turn the TV off, so I said to Tony Dunford, "Don't you think you should turn the TV off, Tony. There is a programme about children on in a minute."

Tony knew what was going to happen and was more than up for it. He was a double murderer himself having knifed one young man in a fight, then killed another one in prison. Of course, as long as it doesn't have anything to do with sex, no proper con objects to anyone killing adults. Without asking anyone, Tony turned the TV off.

The room was very quiet. Burgess just sat there next to his minder oblivious to the hate that was building up in the minds of all the other cons.

Now came the next phase – winding everyone up until someone snapped. I said to Len Willshire, "Have you got any kids, Len."

Len knew his lines, “Yeah, one. A little girl.”

“How do you feel about this animal, then?” I said looking at Burgess. There is a feel to a mob. You get carried by the collective emotion and the more powerful it is the more you go with it. This mood was hate.

“He likes to rape little girls, fuck them up the arse, then strangle them…”

“Charming. Shouldn’t someone strangle him, well kick his bollocks in first…”

The remarks were coming thick and fast and even Burgess picked up the crescendo of venom. His head was jerking from side to side as he looked at each speaker. He had his hands on the side of his chair gripping the frame tightly; he was twitching in his seat. It was going to blow any second. Some hothead was going to attack him and when he did Burgess was getting my knuckles screwed into the back of his neck…as long as the screw couldn’t see me do it. But the screw felt what was happening as acutely as anyone in the room. He stood up without warning and looking not at Burgess but at the seated, baiting cons he said authoritatively, “Out Burgess. Out. Get back to your cell.” The screw was on the ball.

I was still standing by the door and Burgess went past me with the screw following him; there were two others hovering on the landing drawn by the tension. As Burgess left, the fear he’d been showing lifted and he appeared almost nonchalant as he was hustled off to his cell. He obviously felt protected by having screws around him.

I was disappointed that no one had gone for his jugular. Bernie Beauty, another London robber, said to me after things had calmed down, “John, that was a victory. No one got nicked and Gordon will be sick."

I didn't see it like that; Burgess should have been done. Second I knew that Gordon would be furious at seeing his orders countermanded by our intimidation. However, everyone felt slightly humiliated at letting a nonce off the hook and the agreement was that, if it happened again everyone in the wing would get a cup of boiling water, from the boiler downstairs, then on the signal of someone turning the TV room lights off, everyone would do Burgess, then scuttle back to their cells.

The next day the Threes' landing had an air of tension. We all knew we couldn't back out; it did not help that the Twos' cons who used the TV room on their landing were visibly pleased it wasn't on their plate. Charlie Richardson, a Twos' resident, put his own gruesome spoke in when I told him what was going to happen.

"Boiling fat would be better, John," he said. "It clings and, as they try to get it off, they make it worse." He clawed his hands across his face in a chilling simulation of someone trying to relieve the agony. Trust Charlie to plant this phantom of the opera horror. Charlie has a charming, slightly ingratiating manner that makes it easy to forget his enthusiastic support of Fraser's sick theatre.

I chided Charlie for what he was suggesting. "Oh, that's lovely, Chas. We'll all end up with another five (years) apiece. Water we can get away with – but boiling fat! That's like saying I haven't got enough time already, please give me some more." I didn't mention my other objection. Extra time on my sentence would wipe out the only edge I had on Charlie – the two more years he was serving than me.

It was noticeable, though, that no one who frequented the Twos' room offered to join us if Burgess appeared again. That evening no one did any weight–lifting and all the Threes' men came out of their cells holding their mugs as a testimonial to their staunchness. But Burgess decided to seek fresh pastures and went into the Twos' TV room!

I was up on the Threes nursing my mug with the others on the landing when we heard this. There were more than a few grinning faces, including my own, at the way the tables had been turned. It had not gone unnoticed that when the problem broke none of the cons on the Twos had offered to back us. Lots of encouragement and moral support but no offers to *make one* (join in). Although it was unvoiced, everyone knew that if Burgess was badly injured or even killed anyone tied to the attack was upping his sentence. Scalding him left it all to identification with no forensic evidence to complicate matters. Everyone involved knew the score. The relief among the Threes' cons that the ball was out of our court with no obligation to back up the Twos was palpable.

Bernie summed up the mood, "They didn't come up and offer to make one with us, did they? We were going to do him tonight, so now it's their turn." Which was true, but I hadn't been there long enough to become identified with my landing and I felt rather more personal about Burgess than my fellow would-be scalders.

I wandered down onto the Twos and walked past the TV room – it was directly under ours. The room was empty except for Burgess and a screw. I walked into Charlie's cell where there were five of them plotting what to do. They weren't showing much relish for the task. I suppose we were going soft in E-Wing as the screws were off our backs, we didn't have to work and, in our different ways, we were all sloping through our sentences. No one wanted to volunteer for some extra time on their sentence and being banged-up to boot. Even when the key has been thrown away, a con with an easy life still has lots to lose.

I took it upon myself to stiffen the moral fibre. "Well, he's got to be done tonight," I reminded them. "You've got to do what we decided on last night – the boiling water in the face. The chances are no one will be nicked." None of them demurred. As we were the previous evening, they were trapped in the macho prison code. A couple of them went out to get their mugs and I went out to monitor if there were any back–sliders and to watch the action. However, as I passed the TV room, the only person in there was Bondy, another London robber. He was sitting calmly back in an armchair, smoking and watching TV.

"Where's Burgess?" I asked.

"I told him to fuck off or he'd get hurt and he just left and locked himself up." Bondy didn't look at me as he spoke.

"What?" I felt that Burgess had slipped the noose. "But he should be done, he's a sex case."

"'Don't you think I don't know that, John?" he answered calmly and unimpressed. "But the way you're going about it, you'll get everyone nicked. If it's got to be done, then it's got to be done, but not your way. You're just winding everyone up." Bondy was telling me off, but to save my face we could both pretend he wasn't. I wondered whether I should push it. I didn't.

I commented lamely, "Well, someone had to do something." Bondy just grunted. Then some of the other twos people began drifting into the room and we began speculating about what Gordon would get up to next.

Gordon didn't like being thwarted. His first move was to install another TV set for the sex cases on the top landing, the Fours. The screws kindly leaked that it was a better set than either of ours. This tweaked a few exposed nerves. "The governor does love a sex case" became a much heard catchphrase in the next few days, but at least everyone had a new topic to talk about instead of each other. The trouble with long-term convicts is they don't really have anything interesting to do except conduct a guerrilla war with their captors or feud with each other. When the staff get off their back and let them get on with it, the tendency is for them to default to the latter.

I had become friendly with Eddie Richardson, the younger brother of Charlie. Eddie had been a worker for Charlie, cutting up scrap and also scrapping with his fists. A tough guy but not cunning, devious and cruel like his older brother or Fraser. He'd been involved in the torture but not as a prime mover and I found him OK; we'd work out together on the weights, swap newspapers and books or just exchange stories about life outside. However, Eddie like Charlie was a Twos' resident while I was located on the Threes where I also hung out some of the time with the cons up there.

Most long-term cons are losers who have spent their lives getting caught without even the salve of getting away with anything. These are men who have never had any money, any women, anything except a life in prison that often began when they were at school. Despite never receiving any visitors and rarely even a letter, some of these types build up a life in prisons. They acquire a rep perhaps through fighting the system or other cons. Prisons run on violence, so the ones who are good at it tend to emerge as top dogs even if they have never had a bean outside. They are sad cases but they are invariably so bitter and twisted that you can't feel sorry for them; they would stab you in the back for a smouldering dog-end. As they are a fact of life in all long-term prisons, every other con has to come to terms with their existence and the problems living among them poses.

There were a few of these types, mostly lifers, on the Threes and naturally they hated Charlie. I mean everyone disliked Charlie – except those people who were dependent on him – but these state-reared mugs hated him with a vengeance. Mainly because he was rich, had lived it up outside and with his money could still pull some strings out there. They would sit around in the so-called workshop, where no one did anything remotely resembling work, gossiping about other cons. Charlie came to be their favourite subject.

Running down Charlie was easy to do because while he paid lip service to the prison code he flouted every rule in it. It wasn't merely that Charlie had done everything they dreamed about doing but never would, he also attended church, cultivated the priest, fraternised with senior warders and was always up to something that made life easier for Charlie.

Charlie is Charlie: unscrupulous, treacherous and ruthless, so the state-reared lowlife found good cause in scapegoating him for their failed lives. The badmouthing, though, started to incorporate Eddie, which made life uncomfortable for me since I was openly friendly with him.

The poisonous comments began to bug me. When I was present, if they lumped Eddie with Charlie, I occasionally defended him but as they were brothers and had been part of the same torture gang racket I was on my back foot. One day in the Threes' workroom, I said to Lennie, who was part of it, "Look, Eddie is not Charlie and in my book he is OK."

"What, you know he hasn't done Charlie's bidding? Wasn't part of the trials, wasn't there when they tortured George Carnie and Frank pulled his teeth out with pliers..." Lennie was a Londoner who knew a bit more than the other low-life that was part of this verbal lynch mob.

"Well, if that's what you think Len you should tell him," I replied. It was said very mildly but the six people in the room knew I'd upped the ante to close to a challenge. Cons whose only asset is their rep become almost psychic to anything that could erode it. Len didn't answer but one of his two cronies did, a state-reared cockroach named Hilton.

Hilton was serving life as was his mate, Vince "the mince", who were part of Len's cabal. Both of them made up for their weediness by taking to a tool at the first hint of trouble. Hilton said jokingly to no one in particular, "I think someone might."

The jokey tone was to take the sting out of the insinuation but I'd had enough. I stood up and, as I walked out the room, I replied, "I just might do that."

I went down and cornered Eddie out of sight of everyone. I told him what had been going on and how I'd become increasingly irritated by it. He was furious but confused, too, because he not only didn't know what to do but also didn't understand why they were digging him out.

"What are they on about?" he asked, "I don't even know them. The only one I even talk to is Len."

"You have", I replied, "not done any *bird* (prison) before, but nicks are full of cockroaches like that. They hate the screws, themselves and anyone who's had it better than them. And they love setting people at each other's throat. Feuding is the only excitement in their lives. That's what they do." And what I said is true. These are people who even if they could would not escape. The only place they are anybody is in prison.

"What should I do, then?" he asked. "Forget it?"

I didn't want him to forget it as I was as angry as him. "I think you should give 'em a tug (front up someone on the threat of violence). I'll back you up. We can spring 'em. As long as they aren't *tooled up* (carrying a weapon), we can batter the three of 'em. But they'll swallow it. I know they will."

That evening after everyone was unlocked I sauntered down onto the Ones to get the weights out from the storeroom cell. Eddie was floating about but he was up on the Twos clocking me. Lennie and his two mates also came down for a workout and went into the cell where they were stowed to get out a bench and barbell. As soon as they did, I signalled Eddie. He darted down the stairs and strode into the weightlifting room and I followed him. The three of them were just picking up the bench and barbell. They saw that Eddie was steamed up and knew exactly what was going down. I pushed the door to, which had the lock sprung.

Eddie went right into one. He was belligerent and was jabbing his finger at them as he snarled, "You three cunts 'ave been talking about me behind my back. You got anything to say about me, say it to my face." He was snarling and ready to blow.

Lennie held his hands out in appeasement, "What you on about Ed? What's got into you?"

The moment they saw us they knew what was on and why. That was the reality: the ensuing words could sharpen or blur it but the five of us knew that they'd been confronted and backed down.

I said flatly, "I told him what's been said about him. He's a pal of mine and you know I didn't like it." I now started to fudge the way they'd swallowed it, so later they'd have something to salve their wounded pride. "You'd all do the same if I was running down one of your mates."

"The Mince" – he was said to have put a body through an industrial meat mincer – picked up the card I'd thrown him and made a bigger play with it than I liked. He muttered, "Sometimes things are said that don't mean what other people say they mean."

I eyeballed him, "Eddie's the judge of that." But I said it neutrally. I didn't want to rub their nose in it, so that afterwards they'd stew on it and decide that they have to stab one of us to restore face.

Bernie suddenly pushed open the cell door to get at the training gear. I jammed it with my heel and said, "Bernie, we are talking." He left us alone.

Eddie was still raging. He said, "John doesn't lie to me. If it happens again there is gonna be fucking trouble 'cos I am not having it." If it happens again! Eddie had been in enough of these showdowns outside to read the universal body language. He wasn't as raging as he appeared.

Lennie said, "Eddie there has been a bit of a misunderstanding, that's all. No one is trying to mug you off." Bar the talking, it was over.

I lost interest. I called timeout, "Okay, okay. It's a misunderstanding. Let's just forget it. I just wanna have a workout..." We all went back to doing what otherwise we would have been doing. But after this I kept away from the cockroaches and pitched in more with Eddie, virtually deserting the Threes. I also watched my back rather more closely than I had hitherto.

Things settled down for a few weeks, but then came the next Gordon bombshell – a four-page memorandum posted on the notice board on the Ones. It promulgated the new regime that was to be introduced when the new workshop opened in a fortnight. This had been brewing for some time and everyone accepted that the existing regime – no work – was temporary. Prisons regimes have to pretend to work their inmates and most of us had learnt to collude in that illusion.

Of course, a lot of the hang-'em-and-flog-'em brigade see work as a panacea to the problem of prisons, even crime. Every now and again some Tory politician goes on a crusade to do precisely this. It's a cyclical phenomenon and, like the seasons, unstoppable – it has been going on since prisons were built. The package includes making prisoners work harder for its own sake – they have usually seen that prisons are cesspits of idleness – but also to pay for their keep and sometimes to compensate their victims.

Now you can make prisoners work – as long as the stick to make them is heavy enough. China and Russia have their labour camps where cons produce more than they consume. But slave labour is brutal and dehumanising and not really on in a democratic society. And the carrot approach doesn't work either.

The workforce is unskilled, it cannot be allocated productively; security provisions to stop escapes, prevent riots, attacks on staff and by cons on each other will always override and counter sound economic management; finally, the plant necessary to make cons productive is vulnerable to sabotage. In any long-term prison, there is maintenance work and craft-like workshops but industrial prisons are a pipe dream.

Most of us were detailed for the workshop. In addition, a rota system for doing our own cleaning and dish washing was set up. As the wing had started off pretty much like a punishment block with everyone banged up in their cells, all the cleaning had been done by short-termers who came over from the main prison. This provision continued even as the regime was eroded and we were let out of cells more and given the run of the wing. The order that we take over our own cleaning was resented but not rejected – it was customary for cons to do their own cleaning. They did in the other special wings.

It wasn't the dreaded workshop but what went with it that got us hopping about on the hot tin roof: Gordon wanted to regiment what we wore. His new dress code was shoes instead of basketball boots and trainers, no overalls except at work, flannel trousers otherwise, no T-shirts, prison issue shirts to be worn at all times. It was back to the barracks. Bernie looked at all this and began marching about like a demented marionette and shouting like a drill sergeant: "We're in the army now…yes sir, no sir, three bags full sir. Can I 'ave a short–back and sides sir? Left, right, left, right… About turn. At ease…"

Most of us had been there before. Prison staff, as I have already explained, have an obsession with anything military. It's the uniform mentality. Retributionists want the birch and the rope; right wingers want work; Blimps want boot camp. It's the "bring back national service" brigade: anything going to the dogs, conscription will save it.

You can't reason with these people, but the thinking behind their position is senseless. After all, the whole purpose of army training is to mould fit, obedient killers. I mean, if you look at it sensibly, the last thing you should want to do with young criminals is toughen them up or train them to fight. I have always thought that it made much more sense to encourage convicts to be pacifists, hippies or Bohemians or artists. If he'd had society's interests at heart, Gordon should have been applauding our eccentric dress, letting us grow our hair how we liked and making work voluntary.

Alan Greene, the assistant governor, came on the scene more. He was a navy man who had come into the prison service late, so he did not have the usual screw mentality. However, it was his job to sell us the advantages of the new regime but the courtesy and irony with which did it made it pretty plain that he did not believe in what Gordon was up to. He also picked up the mood of the cons, which was openly rebellious. Nonetheless, he clearly had no power either to change the orders or the mind of the man who was responsible for them.

Under pressure from Greene, Gordon did agree to meet us and listen to our objections, so a week before they came into effect we all crowded into the visiting rooms that abutted the end of the wing and waited for him to appear. He walked in flanked on either side by Greene and the Chief Officer. There had been much talk about what we should do when Monday came but nothing concrete had been decided. After they walked in, the Chief took a wooden chair and placed it at the head of the room and Gordon sat down. He and Greene stood to the side and behind him – the scene was a bit like a feudal lord with his advisors confronting a deputation of unruly peasants.

Gordon was about forty-six years old, five feet ten inches in height, slim and a smart dresser – he wore snappy felt hats that gave him a rakish look that went with his nickname "Flash". In fact, this impression was quite misleading as he was a rigid, uncompromising man in both manner and character. He sat down primly and waited aloofly until the hubbub had subsided. He spoke in an authoritarian tone, which brooked no concessions. As Eddie had with the three cockroaches, he threw down the gauntlet at us. It was either obey or suffer the consequences.

He spoke precisely and without inflexion: "I have called this meeting to enable you to put any questions to me to clear up any misunderstanding or confusion about the new orders that come into effect on Monday." Actually, the regulations were crystal clear – there were no misunderstandings or confusion, only objections. "Do any of you wish to ask a question?"

There were more comments than questions but everything raised went to the dress regulations not the new working arrangements. There were a lot of attempts to draw him into debating the merits of the dress code, which drew on the widely-publicised report by a committee for penal reform which had recently recommended that security-wing prisoners should be regimented as little as possible. The committee's worthies had actually identified dress as one area where freedom of choice should prevail. Those cons who referred to this clearly thought that they had Gordon snookered, but he had come along to lay the law down not justify it.

His face composed and unchanging, he replied, "The rules are laid down by head office and it's not my function to justify them." Sometimes when the questioner went to a specific matter like wearing a T-shirt, Gordon would read out the appropriate section in his memorandum about prison issue shirts, noting that it complied with head office's policy.

Some of the hotheads were openly defiant but he did not register any irritation or anger. However, anger was building up among some of them and I became worried that someone might start ranting and raving and threaten to clump him or, worse, try to. The heavy mob would have been waiting off stage for any trouble. That is the way these things are done.

I hadn't asked a question mainly because some of the cons regarded me as opinionated and arrogant. They all knew about the mess I'd made at Chelmsford; then there was also the way I'd set up the confrontation in which I sided with Eddie. But I did intervene if only to head off some hothead who, if he flared up, would precipitate an immediate crackdown. I just said matter-of-factly to Gordon, "So you're rigid about these dress regulations, Governor?'

"Yes, I am," he replied.

I stood up and said to Eddie more than anyone, "Well, there's no further point in continuing the meeting." Eddie got up too, then Charlie, which facilitated a consensus and the meeting broke up.

At least now we could plan our response rather than being pushed into an impromptu showdown, by some hothead erupting, thereby denying us even the chance of getting a few licks in before we went under. Opinion hardened around a protest rather than a passive refusal to obey the regulations or to smash up our cells or do something that the staff could easily handle.

We had very few options. Some of the diehards wanted a "dirty protest" in the Fraser mould whereby everyone shat in their pot and dumped it over a screw. That was talked about but not implemented. Thankfully. I am just not an excrement man. The enthusiasm with which many prisoners take to buggering their weaker brethren, for example, has never been something I shared. Sodomy is both messy and smelly but one consequence of this is that its devotees become inured to faeces. The only place I like to see shit is coiled up in the bottom of the lavatory pan before I flush it. Unfortunately, a lot of long-term prisoners, like public school boys, develop an unhealthy interest in the anal passage and all things scatological.

By about Friday, the projected protest had taken the definite form of storming the administration offices, then barricading ourselves inside. Where the plan originated I have no idea but it was by far the best of what was on offer and was agreed upon by all and sundry.

Chapter 3
The riot

The office was part of a new two-storey building grafted onto the end of the wing. The lower half consisted of two visiting rooms reached by the wing exits down on the Ones; the second storey could only be reached by a steel gate at the end of the Twos' landing. This gate opened inward into a small passageway about twelve feet long, and halfway down it the door of the office opened on the left and the door of the chapel on the right. In the chapel was an altar about eight feet long, like a massive wooden box, and rows of chairs; the office contained four big steel filing cabinets and some office furniture. The windows of the office and the chapel were bullet-proof and barred, so that if we could get in through the gate and erect a barricade in the passage we were virtually impregnable unless they resorted to tear gas.

The problem of getting in there wasn't all that difficult either. All the cells were fitted with piped radio, as in hospitals, but there were only two outlets to plug the supplied earphones into. Not everyone had their own radio and it was common for a con to ask the staff to tune in another station. This meant a screw unlocking the steel gate at the end of the Twos, then going into the office where the main radio was located and setting another station. Generally, this task fell to one of the senior screws, a Principal Officer, and quite often they left the gate open while tuning the set.

This procedure and the lay-out of the office more or less dictated the plan. It meant that everyone would have to be in the Twos' TV room or in cells near the gate. Then someone would have to ask the Principal Officer to change one of the stations, once he was inside everyone would have to dash for the gate. Those in front would have the task of grabbing the screw, taking his keys and then locking the gate after chucking him out onto the landing. We did not want to take him hostage as that could provoke a much more determined counter-attack and could also lead to outside charges being preferred rather than the offence being handled internally. While no one minded losing remission, the prospect of another sentence on top of what we were already serving was viewed with alarm by most of us. Securing the key from the Principal Officer was crucial as it was the only one in the wing. While the screws secured a duplicate elsewhere in the prison, we would be able to erect our barricade at leisure.

Once the plan was conceived, we hardly spoke of anything else. The wing was throbbing with excitement and an almost carnival atmosphere developed. What whipped up the fever was the knowledge that inside the office were our personal files headed: 'Prisoner's Record'. Everything that for all our convicted lives had been laboriously and lovingly and secretly compiled about us. Reports, confiscated letters, disciplinary offences...my own file was massive with well over 2,000 pages of foolscap going back to when I first came into prison as a 16-year-old. All convicts hate this dossier as it details everything the authorities know about them and can be accessed by any warder or member of staff. Warders idly read it when one is being transferred as it accompanies every inmate as he is moved around the prison system. It's Big Brother's documentary cosh.

The only con in the wing who was not party to all this was John Whitney who was malingering in bed with bronchitis. A sickly, weedy man, Whitney was one of life's walking wounded, ever poorly but always desperately drawing on a scrawny roll-up. He had been the driver for a couple of stick-up gunmen, Harry Roberts and John Duddy, who had been robbing betting offices in the West London area. Roberts had been in the British Army in Malaya in the 1950s and as well as learning how to handle firearms he had acquired a taste for killing prisoners on the orders of his officers. In prison, he liked to gloat over the people he'd killed.

In 1966, the three of them had been parked up preparing to rob a betting shop in Shepherd's Bush but a passing Q-car clocked them, stopped, then two plain clothes detectives came over to Whitney who was at the wheel. The car's tax disc was out of date, but what interested DC David Wombwell was a holdall bag nestling between the two front seats. He pointed to the bag and asked, "What's in the bag?"

Harry Roberts, who was in the back seat answered, "Me work tools. It's me toolbag." Roberts had already decided that he would kill the three of them if he was ordered to open the toolbag. He'd already served seven years for robbing an old lady.

The detective said to Roberts, "Well let's have a look then." Roberts put his hand inside the bag and pulled out a .38 automatic. He shot Wombwell in the head.

His partner, DS Christopher Head, ran off actually passing the Q-car and its driver before Roberts got him in the back. Roberts had given a gun to Duddy who joined him outside the car to fire at the escaping detective. As the ballistic evidence was not definitive, Duddy always thought that he had shot the running detective. Roberts never told him that he'd killed Head, which always made him chuckle. Duddy turned to religion before dying in prison, never knowing the truth. After seeing Head go down, Roberts then fired into the Q-car killing the driver. They all received life with a recommendation from the trial judge that they serve 30 years before being considered for release on licence.

Anyway, I was wandering around the wing, looking for any distraction to take my mind off tomorrow's performance. I saw John Duddy, who had been nicked with Whitney, and asked him if Jack – although named John Whitney, he was called Jack – was going to make one with us. He just said, "I doubt it. After Harry Roberts, his nervous system collapsed and that's not all that collapsed, I think. But ask him. You never know until you ask." I should have twigged that if his mate hadn't asked there was little point in me doing it. But the deal was that anyone who didn't want to make one could bang himself up Sunday evening and leave the rest of us to it. So I made myself busy to invite Whitney.

I went into his cell where he was sitting up in bed talking to another one of his mates. The air was thick with Black Beauty tobacco, which only prisons stocked, Whitney was puffing away as if acrid smoke was a newly-discovered cure for respiratory diseases. I said, "Jack, you know we are gonna stage a protest tomorrow over Gordon's new regime?"

A look of alarm spread over his face, "No. I didn't know. No one told me."

I explained what the score was and said, "You're gonna be with, ain't yer?"

He blanched and flopped back onto his pillow. I dread to think what was going on inside his underpants. He had a quick drag to stiffen the moral fibre and replied, "Tomorrow night. In the office. I dunno…err I ain't feeling too good. I'd like to but I can't promise. I'll just see how I am."

"Well, you look alright to me," I replied.

"It's in the lungs, John. I can hardly breathe." His mate, Chris, was listening to the exchange with a grin on his face. I just shrugged and said I'd see them later. Predictably, Whitney suffered a spectacular relapse, by the afternoon the lungs just about supported life but not coherent speech. He went under the blanket and even had his grub served bedside.

But this didn't bother the rest of us and Whitney's decline became another running joke while we went ahead with our plans. We decided to mount our invasion on Sunday evening in the dying embers of the old regime. Anderson, a young London robber, was elected to get the PO (Principal Officer) in to retune the radio, as this was a regular late evening touch of his.

On Saturday night, about 8 o'clock, eighteen of the twenty-two of us who had declared in started to drift down to the Twos' TV room. Some of us spread the load a bit by drifting along the cells near the gate but there were about fourteen of us in the TV room. There were buckets of water, trays of bread pudding, boiled eggs wrapped up in towels and whatever fare people had salvaged from the last few prison meals. It was all

Mug shots of Charlie Richardson at the time of his arrest in 1967

hidden away under the chairs in the TV room. I was conscious that this was another one of those could-go-wrong jobs with outside charges if any screws got hurt. In the negotiations concerning who would do what, I had detailed myself off for being part of the team supplying the barricade builders with furniture from the chapel. In the vernacular, I was making sure that I wouldn't be in the frame if outside charges were preferred.

About a quarter past eight, Andy sauntered down to the office on the Ones and asked the PO to change the radio. They both came up and went through the gate. Roy Hall who after Fraser used to be Charlie Richardson's favourite torturer was watching from the TV room; the rest looking like they were on the starting grid of a seaside handicap, crouched on the landings out of sight of the screws, holding buckets and trays. Everyone knew that as soon as it was off, the screws would steam up onto the Twos and attempt to pick off the back markers. I for one wasn't going to be last through the gate.

Roy was leaning on the railings of the Twos looking suitably bored. As Andy and the screw went into the office, he hissed, "They're in there but he's locked the gate behind him." Roy said, grinning. A bit of a cheeky-chappie, Roy always delighted in anything that went wrong. With fourteen of us lined up for the cavalry charge down the landing and into the office, it was likely to turn into a stampede. But it all depended, of course, on the gate being open. If we couldn't get in the office, then D-Day was off.

Dennis Stafford, who had gunned a business rival down in Newcastle but despite admitting it to all and sundry had one of those miscarriage of justice bandwagons rolling on his conviction, said grimly, "We can't call it off now."

Charlie took up Dennis' call. He was pacing up and down in the middle of the room and took it upon himself to rally the troops. "Come on," he said round at everyone. "What are we fucking about for? This is no good. We've got to get into that office." He was shaking and his face was flushed. He had the look of someone who is whipping himself up into a frenzy of resolution. But people who try to will something to happen are incapable of thinking on their feet. They often jump the gun and carry everyone over the top with them.

"We're going to get into that office," he said, staring wild-eyed at everyone. I wondered if he might suddenly dash out of the TV room in blind determination and trip a disaster.

I said, "Leave it out, Chas. You'll *noise* (ruin) the whole thing." I turned to Eddie who was looking at his brother like a faithful Labrador. "Eddie," I appealed, "for fuck's sake calm him down. The gate's locked. We can't get in there."

It was obvious to anyone who had worked on the pavement (robbing security vans and banks) what needed to be done. Someone had to spring the PO as he came out of the gate with Andy. Grab his keys before he locked the gate, which would be the cue for the charge. The obvious candidate was Andy, but he was about eight stone nothing and not up to anything physical.

"Someone has to cop for the PO as he comes out the gate with Andy," I said. With the solution posed to the problem, all the agiprops calmed down. But there were no volunteers for the mission.

Roy shifted the focus, "They're coming out the office. He's locked the gate. He's waiting there. Andy's going to have a listen in his cell, I think, to make sure it's tuned in OK. The PO's by the gate."

Inside the TV room, I saw Andy as he walked across my line of vision. His cell was virtually opposite the TV room but on the other side of the landing. Andy said to Roy for the benefit of any earwigging screws, who were lounging around on the Ones, "I'm going to test it, Roy." We all heard him too.

Roy said, "Make sure you get it right, then. I'm sick and tired of you fucking up that radio."

Everyone could feel it all slipping away from them at this unexpected turn of events.

Charlie had calmed down. He appealed to me, "John, you do it, will you? You've got the sense. Someone else is bound to fuck it up."

I knew he was working me, but my vanity was too greedy to be able to resist. But as I went with his suggestion, I could see an edge for me – I would be a front runner in making entry into the office! I didn't fancy being coshed from behind as in all probability the back markers would be. I replied, "Alright. I'll go down and spring him as Andy comes out with him." I said to Hilton, "You grab his keys, and lock that gate after I've pushed him out and everyone's inside." Hilton nodded his agreement – he'd nominated himself to do this in the original scheme anyway. For the purposes of the demo, all the cockroaches, including Hilton, had been temporarily upgraded to 'one of your own'.

Andy came out of his cell, walked across the bridge catwalk and stopped next to Roy. I came out and joined them. Andy said, "He's locked the poxy gate. What shall I do?"

I said, "Go back in with him to retune it. When you come out and he's unlocked the gate, grab him to stop him locking it again. I'll be right on you as you do."

Andy looked at me knowing that he'd be the patsy if I let him down. "You're sure?"

I knew the look. Andy was going out on a limb – would I back him up? I struck on the deal, "I'll be there, Andy. Don't worry."

He sauntered off down the landing towards the office explaining to the PO that it just needed a touch of re-tuning. After locking the gate, the PO and him both disappeared into the office. I strolled casually out onto the bridge and onto the other side of the landing, then walked down to Les' cell, which was about eight feet from the gate. There were no screws on the Twos' landing at all: they were all on the Threes or Ones. My own tunnel vision, however, was now blinkering me to clues. I didn't *tumble* (work out) that the screws fancied something was going down and were geared up for when it happened.

I walked in. Les was there with Tony Dunford. I quickly explained the change of plan, then I stood out of sight by the cell door ready for the starter's gun. I heard Andy and the PO approach the gate, the keys jingling as the PO unlocked it. Then I heard the PO say, "Oy, what the..."

I came out of the traps and copped for the PO as he struggled out of Andy's arms. I held his arms tightly against his side, making sure that he couldn't use his keys to lock the gate. Screws are not called turnkeys for nothing; some of them can lock a door quicker than a hooker can peel on a condom.

As always I was reassuring but firm. "You won't get hurt," I said. "Just behave yourself and you'll be OK." Meanwhile the others were all stampeding along the catwalk on my left, Les and Tony had already gone past us. Hilton reached me first and ripped the keys off the PO's belt. As everyone started going through the gate, which was only a little wider than the average door, I released the PO and started pushing him out. But he didn't need much pushing. He waded through the incoming bodies like a salmon swimming upstream against a heavy current. A couple of the cons gave him a clump as they went past him but the only thing he cared about was not joining us in the office.

As the last of our lot were getting in, he made it onto the landing but then I saw the vanguard of the heavy mob, steaming down both sides of the Twos. They were holding big riots sticks in their hands and shouting – I realised with a jerk what I had missed when I walked from the TV room to Les' cell. The heavy mob had been laid on for the expected demo. Later on I discovered that they had been waiting in the visiting rooms all evening. What they hadn't worked out was our target, even though the office was directly above where they were plotting up.

We closed the gate. The PO was standing out on the landing, looking dazed and dishevelled. The heavy mob hit the gate, jabbing their sticks through at us, just as Hilton got the key in the lock and turned it. They were sick with frustration. The altar came rocketing out of the chapel and was slammed up against the gate. I went in there, smashing furniture to buttress the back of the altar; others were doing the same with chairs from the office. Soon the whole passageway that led from the gate to the doors that led off to the left into the office and the right into the chapel was jammed with steel filing cabinets, furniture, and even the doors of the chapel and the office.

Bondy, a 15 years man, was in charge of building the barricade. Afterwards someone described him as a "tower of strength". A six-foot powerhouse of a man, Bondy built up the barricade so well that it would have needed a bulldozer to break it down. The screws kept poking their sticks through the gaps in the furniture as Bondy constructed it but he kept to his task despite a few blows. Next, a screw appeared with a duplicate key for the gate. However, even when they unlocked it, the door hardly budged as they pushed against it. The next minute some of the screws appeared with a couple of long crowbars and attempted to lever back the gate, but as it opened inward and the barricade was rock solid it didn't shift appreciably.

Meanwhile, Charlie and his lot had been ripping off from the office walls some metal piping that protected the electric wiring. With a bit of twisting, these lengths were fashioned into five foot "pokes". Charlie organised a poking party to discourage the screws who were still trying to lever open the gate. Charlie's poke corps was four-strong and whenever the screws got too enterprising they would wiggle through gaps in the barricade and fend them off. Charlie was also having a rare time taunting them.

"You Geordie cunts; you're the thickest screws in the country. Thick as pigshit, which is what you eat…"

Some of them responded in kind usually shaking a big riot stick. "Let's see if you say that when you come out Richardson. You've got to come out sometime, lad. And when you do…"

I made myself conspicuously absent from all this, I had done my bit of front line work. I stayed in the chapel, smashing furniture for Bondy, who was still busy shoring up the defences. Although the barricade was up to the ceiling and now past the entrances to the office and chapel, it was easy to clamber through gaps in it to get to and from the two rooms. The screws kept pushing and poking at Bondy for about an hour, but within half an hour it was virtually impregnable. I then went over into the office.

The noise was like I was in the stands at the Arsenal just after they'd scored. Everyone was talking and shouting at once. There were records and paper and photos scattered all over the place. Stafford was over by the window talking over the telephone with a *Daily Mirror* reporter whom he knew from the outside. Dennis had owned a night-club, lived with a jazz singer and loved the limelight. He was like Charlie in respect of having lived much more than most of us. I flopped down beside him. He was saying, "It's me,

Dennis, Dennis Stafford." The reporter wouldn't believe him.

Dennis told him what they had done the last time they'd met, but the reporter still wouldn't believe him. He made Dennis give him the number, so that he could check it and ring back. About three minutes later the phone rang – it was the reporter. Dennis tried to tell him about the riot but he had to appeal for some hush. It was utter pandemonium. Everyone was flushed and excited, some of them so high that I thought maybe they'd soon be rolling about on the floor in a kind of religious ecstasy. The office was about twelve foot by eighteen foot and most of us were congregated inside it.

Dennis was briefing the reporter and trying to persuade him to give us a reasonable write-up. He stressed that it was a non-violent protest aimed at alerting the Home Secretary to the terrible conditions in the hell-hole. There was a lot of stuff about how the warders terrorised and regularly beat us up. It was the usual propaganda. I got bored with listening to him, so I got up and started to look for my record.

Some of the others were frantically doing the same, worried that they would not be able to destroy theirs before the screws mounted a counter-attack. The office floor was a mass of smashed furniture and scattered papers with people searching around for their files. Someone shouted to me over the bedlam, "I've got your record, John." He dumped it on the radio. I went over and picked it up with both hands, then found a bit of wall that I could sit against while I went through it. A few others had got theirs and were greedily ripping their sins into oblivion. I mentally made a note of one or two who weren't showing the choicest bits to anyone. But most of them were reading out passages to each other that were either funny or portrayed them as far worse than they actually were.

There was a lot of speculation about what the screws would do to get us out and every few minutes or so, there'd be a scream from a sentinel on the barricade calling the pokers to repel boarders. There'd be a rush down to the passage, but most of the calls were false alarms and everyone would quickly come back to the task of reading and destroying their record.

A bit over an hour into the mutiny, Gordon appeared on the scene. There was a shout, "Gordon's here." This caused a Gadarene rush to the barricade to bawl him out; everyone, including me, was screaming and cursing him in a torrent of obscenity. My own reaction was as uncontrolled as everyone else's. He had as much chance of negotiating a settlement as the public hangman. This vituperative chorus persuaded him that his peacemaking stock was zilch and he left without saying anything. I watched his face. We were vermin to him but the crescendo of hate that just his presence orchestrated seemed to unsettle him. Although he was composed, his eyes registered defeat. He'd blundered and he knew it. Given that the staff knew we were likely to stage a protest, we should never have been able to commandeer our office beachhead.

I went back into the office, grabbed my record again, then went back to Dennis, who between talking to reporters – he'd located others – was still screaming out for quiet. The noise would abate, but hysteria makes for a poor memory and the racket would soon build up again. Dennis gave me the phone and I had a natter to the reporter. I told him about a screw who had just said to me through the barricades, "You're going to get some stick when you come out." He took that down, then Charlie started to bend his ear.

We got bored with reporters, so Dennis rang up his girlfriend. He was chatting away to her when I remembered that I should find Burgess's record and make sure that no one ripped it up by mistake. It was a celebration: everyone was laughing and congratulating each other; by popular and unanimous acclaim this was a coup. There was a rota for the phone now. I felt a bit out of it as I couldn't remember anyone's number. This went on for another hour, until someone rang the prison and told them that we had access to a phone and were briefing the press. The phone bill must have come to a bomb.

They cut off the phone, the heat and electricity just before the ten o'clock news – we'd tuned in the radio to Radio 4 to listen. Not being able to hear a broadcast about our exploits disappointed us. Everyone began to settle down and the noise subsided; the screws seemed to have packed in for the night. I got hold of my record and Burgess', then by the light that came through the windows from the floodlights outside, I began to read mine carefully. I discovered that outside I was a member of the 'Richardson gang'. I showed this to Eddie and to Charlie, whom I'd never known until I came to Durham; they both boggled at it.

There was a lot of this kind of thing. But I was surprised at how little insight anyone had gleaned into my character, personality or motives. They'd had me in their cells on and off since I was sixteen for 9 years, hundreds of people had filed thousands of reports, yet they knew nothing about me. It was gratifying in one way to know that they hadn't got a bead on me but in another it was disappointing. After all, these were the official experts on criminality and this record had cost a fortune to compile, yet it was worth no more than what I turned it into – a pile of confetti. It was kind of shocking really.

I had expected, at least, to find something out that would make me think. I had failed spectacularly as a criminal. Yet despite being above average intelligence I had shown myself incapable of either learning from my mistakes or changing my game. Even I was mystified why in the face of all my convictions and long sentences I hadn't managed to stop getting caught or, failing that, become law-abiding. The germs of what I was later to do – analyse what I was like and why I became a criminal – were sown by this dossier of garbage.

The priests had contributed to it. I have been an atheist since I was young and, as much as any religion mattered to me, I disliked Christianity. I had never therefore engaged in conversations with priests either in or outside prison. They were as alien to me as I was to them. But there was still a report by one prison chaplain in my record. He'd barged into my cell at Chelmsford, assuring me that he'd not come to convert me, but "just to see if you're alright". We'd spoken for five minutes about generalities, but out of that he'd composed a character study that defined me as a confirmed criminal. Of course, I was a confirmed criminal but he didn't know that; what he'd done was recycle the opinions and assessments of others. His report did not bother me, only confirmed my resolve not to talk to men of the cloth.

A lot of the other cons, though, did talk to priests and some, like Charlie, even went to church. What these were finding out as they read their records were that the priests and chaplains had taken part in the assessment process. Consequently, they were reading in their records what they had told clerics in confidence or in private, which predictably outraged and infuriated them. Such was the head of steam it generated, I had to stifle my amusement. But the upshot of all this was that someone selected the chapel as a temporary khazi and, as a few bowels were already making demands, it was quickly and enthusiastically christened. Charlie made a few dissenting noises, asking the shitters to use the end of the barricade corridor, but he was ignored.

I read Burgess' record, and the psychiatric report on him, the details of his family, and the fact that he was suspected of another murder in the same village. I should have given no more credence to what was written about him than its counterpart about me but, of course, I didn't. While it was propaganda about me, it was gospel about him. I also discovered that he had a glass eye.

Someone else had Brady's record and he read out a transcript of one of the tapes they had found in his home. It was of a little girl whose fingers he was cutting off with garden shears because she would not go down on him. Everything went a deathly quiet; my viscera writhed in nausea. The little girl was appealing to Brady's girlfriend, Myra Hindley, and in the midst of her agony calling to her, "Mummy, please stop him!" There is nothing to say. The office went very quiet, the high spirits dampened by the cold, clammy presence of evil.

A lot of cons make a hobby in prison of making sex cases' lives a misery – I am moderate compared with some of them. When the demo was originally being discussed, a few of us had wanted to take the wing over for long enough to get Brady and Burgess into the office before we erected the barricade. It meant being able to block the entrances at both ends of the wing for at least ten minutes, but we couldn't think how to do it. Of course, as the heavy mob were at the ready, if we'd tried we'd have been battered to a pulp. But if we had secured the wing, they would both have died that night, probably as painfully as their victims.

I didn't want to read Brady's record, but I fished out some of his letters to Myra Hindley that had been stopped. They were intelligently written – much better than the reports on him by prison staff. The letters were steeped in hatred: he hated anyone around him as much as he saw them returning it in kind. Paranoia, I suppose. Prisoners like us were "ignorant peasants", children were "maggots" and so on. The fact that he is abnormal does not mean he is not responsible for his actions. He clearly knew what he was doing, had the choice of not doing it but chose to go ahead. I don't understand – and nor do I want to – people who take a so-called principled stand against capital punishment. It is like pacifism – that's anyone's prerogative but I don't respect it and I am not interested in their arguments. I don't know where the cut off point for capital punishment is, but men who repeatedly kidnap, torture and kill children are, in my opinion, on the wrong side of it.

Yet, even as I say this, I know that the life Brady is forced to lead will never allow any alleviation of his misery. He is too self-conscious to find the sanctuary of insanity. He will go a long way on hatred, but eventually it will burn itself out. He is too intelligent to sink into protective apathy, and when the hate goes he won't he able to support the strain of having no emotional outlet, no friendship, no family, nothing except his correspondence with Hindley. He had already undergone a long and debilitating hunger strike to try to force the Home Office to allow them to visit each other. He has nothing and no one: no future, no hope, no ideology to lean on except nihilism. When the hate burns itself out, the only emotion left to him will be guilt. Guilt rather than misery will get him in the end. He will commit suicide.

This incident marred the picnic; afterwards nothing was the same. But there were still some laughs. Charlie had been cultivating a screw and, so he thought, getting a sympathetic ear for the wrongs done to him by wicked policemen and lying witnesses. He discovered from his record that the screw was a slip-in. He had been given the brief of winning Charlie's confidence and reporting everything he could find out. The reports he made were really the exception that proved the rule that all screws are stupid. This prison warder had written down that…"Richardson is self-centred…completely unrepentant. Feels everyone is fair game to be used and has no qualms about doing it. Is continually trying to establish his innocence with me and enlist my agreement with his running down of the staff." It was bang on.

Charlie's outrage at this betrayal drew Eddie into reading the reports over his shoulder. We were all stretched out on the floor, sitting up against the walls; I was next to Eddie. He normally deferred to his older brother but, on this occasion, even he could not resist rubbing it in. "John," he said to me gleefully, "you've got to read this about Chas." Charlie was speechless. He was overcome by a sense of betrayal, and too astonished even to be angry. I got up a bit so I could read some of it over his other shoulder and I just began laughing out loud. This helped Charlie recover his voice. Shaking his head in disbelief, he muttered, "Imagine it! That rat. All the time he was coming to my cell, he was at it. I can't believe it! I just can't credit it! They're paid to reform us and this is what they do."

Even worse was the priest. Charlie had been working on him as well to convince him that he had been *fitted-up* by the Yard (framed by Scotland Yard) and that he was the victim of an elaborate conspiracy. The priest's reports were as bad as the friendly screw's. When Charlie read these reports, he was so outraged that even he joined the procession into the chapel shithouse.

Everyone was reading out any choice bits about themselves that could enhance their reputations. I did too but, as even the most timorous lambs were branded as fearsome, psychopathic tearaways, none of it, once you thought about it, inflated your reputation. Some of them were so pleased to find anyone who thought they were hard cases they visibly blossomed that night; you could see the regretful look in their eyes as they tore up the choicer sections of their records.

Someone came across Whitney's record and gave it to John Duddy who started reading it out aloud. We discovered that Whitney's bronchial condition and the collapse of his lower alimentary canal paled before his treachery. No wonder he had not wanted to join us in the demo. The record detailed his complaints about not being rewarded for the help he'd given the police in getting Roberts and Duddy. He had been going on about the injustice of drawing the same 30 year recommendation as Duddy and Roberts. One assistant prison governor dubbed him a "jackal of a man", which was rather more restrained than Duddy's verdict after he'd finished reading the file. Whitney's record joined the "not to be destroyed" ones of Burgess and Brady.

Most of us dossed down quietly when the record session was over, but some of them were so stimulated by the coup we had staged that they went on prowling round in what was almost a victory dance. A guy called Terry was prowling around smashing everything that hadn't already been smashed and taking a demonic delight in doing so. "Look at him, John. You can see all the hatred oozing out of him." Eddie and I watched it. "They're gone, John, ain't they? Look at 'em; they've done too much *bird* (time)." Some of them had home-made weapons stuck in their belts and were strutting round the room like pirates on a captured ship: "This is the high spot of their life, John, they'll live off this for the rest of their bird. For once they have got back at the system."

At times, Eddie could be spot on.

It gave me the giggles. Eddie had only done six months before his current sentence of fifteen years. It was all a novelty to him. He still hadn't realised how even long term convicts are mostly inadequates who have never had a life. They start off petty juvenile delinquents but the screws fill them full of hate; they go out and inflict it back on society; come back with more time...it is a vicious cycle that ends up with violent robbery or even murder. They're irremediably anti-social but not evil.

In the early hours of the morning we had a sing-song. The most popular song was *Maybe it's because I'm a Londoner*. Charlie appointed himself choirmaster and he went wild, his fists keeping time with the beat, his eyes glistening, leading everyone on when it flagged: "Maybe it's because…" I didn't know what he was up to. I always delighted in watching, even studying Charlie, but I never fully understood him.

At about three or four in the morning we went to sleep. Occasionally a screw would throw a stone at the window and the bang and reverberation would wake us up, but by then we'd got tired of cursing them and we would lapse back into slumber. Even the eccentrics settled down, everyone was dozing when I was woken by a tumultuous clatter at the barricade. A voice shouted, "They're coming in!" Panic stations at your lowest ebb; everyone staggered up to man the barricades.

Roy Hall was in hysterics. "You should have seen your faces!" he said, all bright and bushy-tailed. I didn't appreciate the joke and collapsed bleary-eyed onto my bit of office carpet and got my head down again without the energy to join in the slagging off that Roy was still getting.

In the morning I was the first one to climb on the barricade and look at the wing. As I looked down at the Ones I saw a sight that was enough to provoke Lord Longford: my bespoke hate-figure, Burgess, was on his hands and knees scrubbing the floor. It hadn't taken the screws long to get him out of his kennel.

"You dirty little one-eyed groveller!" I screamed. The wing was fairly quiet and the noise echoed round. Burgess nearly knocked his bucket over, screws came running out of the PO's office on the ones and some of my lot came up to the barricade to investigate what was happening. Burgess looked stranded and exposed, his good eye bobbing up and down. A screw ordered him round the corner of the L of the wing out of our sight. This pacified us a bit and we returned to our domain.

Riot still from the film *McVicar.*

About 11 am, Assistant Governor Greene came round and Roy had a talk with him through the barricade. Roy just said we weren't coming out unless Gordon's new regime was rescinded. Greene made encouraging noises but he had no power to negotiate anything and Roy came back in to report the conversation.

In response, Stafford and Tony Dunford started drawing up a petition outlining our grievances. The noise had built up again and they found it difficult to concentrate. Also people were doing the oddest things. Les, who was about forty-five, and had a heart condition was swinging on a length of flex he'd got dangling from the ceiling and uttering blood-curdling whoops. Every now and then Charlie would lead a poking expedition to the barricade to jab through the furniture and bars at any screw who was foolish enough to stand near the gate.

I decided to pick up the discarded petition and

finish it. I stated our case, as diplomatically as possible, laying great stress on the non-violent nature of our protest. That claim hardly squared with copping for the PO and jabbing at screws with the pokes but it'd been relatively peaceful. There was a lot of placatory twaddle about how we realised that by our actions we had forfeited any rights we might have in the matter. Yet, again and again, I came back to how Gordon's obsession with regimenting us had whipped up our grievances. It was something to do but, when I had finished, I was rather proud of it especially with all the long words it contained.

I read it out to everyone, translating some of the big words for the thickies. For once, it became quiet; the petition was unanimously accepted and Greene was summoned. Roy handed it out to him on the end of a 'poke'. Later that afternoon, about five, Greene came back and spoke to Roy. He told him a prison director, Bainton, had arrived specially from the Home Office and wished to talk to us, or preferably a spokesman. Tony Dunford was elected to represent us, as he had known Bainton as a prison governor.

Soon after Bainton appeared, and Tony talked to him through the barricade. Bainton said that he had read our statement of grievances and, while he wasn't going to bargain with us, he assured us that they would be given very serious consideration. He managed to convey without really saying so that the longer we took to come out, the less serious the consideration would be.

He badly wanted us out; that was clear from the part of the discussion I could hear from the office door. Tony asked him to come back in an hour's time. We all settled down for a parley. I wanted out. The larder was depleted and there was no water left – the latter meant we only had about four days of rebellion left. Quite apart from all this, there was a terrible stench drifting over from the chapel, nor did there seem to be any falling off of the number of visitors it was attracting. I have already mentioned how many prisoners develop powerful scatological leanings and clearly some of the shirt-lifting contingent found the atmosphere stimulating.

Tony had told us that, as governors go, Bainton was okay and a man of principle. My argument to the assembly was that quickly surrendering to the Home Office envoy would make him look good and Gordon bad. We wouldn't be coming out under threat, or by Hobson's choice; we should be coming out reasonably and rationally, something that Gordon had not been able to persuade us to do. This must, I argued, only improve what chances there were of the Home Office taking a look at Gordon's policies. Bainton was offering us as good an olive branch as we could get in the circumstances. With delay it could only wither.

At first I was in a minority but gradually even the irrational ones were won over by the import of our lack of water. After an hour or so a majority came over to surrendering our beachhead, but there were still six never-say-dies. Charlie, of course, being one. Three of the six were hard-core fanatics who I am sure would have died in there. For some long term prisoners, the only purpose they know or have or even want in life is to rebel against the prison system. Charlie had his own unfathomable motives while the other two were opportunists concerned with their reputation: they saw the edge of being able to boast later about their uncompromising stance. However, we were a democratic forum and by the time the vote was taken everybody had agreed to abide by the majority decision.

Bainton was summoned and Tony demanded that on surrender we should be allowed to have a meal and that we should not lose any of our cell privileges like radio or tobacco. Bainton didn't concede immediately as he knew only too well that the warders would be outraged by this. But he wanted us out and, doubtless, he was champing at the bit to leave Gordon and HMP Durham. He agreed.

I made myself conspicuous in the dismantling of the barricades – authorities are always on the lookout for ringleaders to make an example of. This is an integral part of the mindset of those who run prisons. We emerged before a battery of magistrates and screws, then three at a time, we stripped, bathed, changed our clothes and collected dinner from a hot-plate on the Ones. A few of the screws had gone the rounds of the cells smashing record players, ripping up letters and photos, burning private towels and so on. Luckily they hadn't been into mine.

About a week later the visiting committee came to adjudicate on the offences committed. Thankfully, the PO whom Andy grabbed hadn't recognised me and he was the only one charged with assault. Along with the others I was charged with mutiny and destroying government property.

The first guy to go in, Terry Coutts, explained he had just come out of his cell, got swept up in a mad rush and, in spite of trying desperately to extricate himself, was swept into the office against his will. Once there, the others wouldn't let him go even though he pleaded to be let out. He said that he wanted to call everyone in the office as witnesses to that effect. Whether the magistrates gave him points for effrontery or they couldn't face hearing 17 other cons lie their heads off for him, they acquitted.

When Terry jubilantly announced his news along the cell window grapevine, I decided to put on my barristers wig. I once defended myself on a charge of robbery at the Old Bailey and earned myself a disagreement on the first trail and 8 years on the second. My co-defendant got five years, which rather took away the shine of my first outing at the bar. Nonetheless, after Terry's acquittal on the mutiny charge, I rather fancied that I could bamboozle three Durham magistrates. I invented this terribly complicated story of duress, which depended upon the fact that the Prison Records had been destroyed.

When I appeared before them, I gave a ringing "Not Guilty" in answer to the charges. I established two things from the PO who gave evidence about the facts of the riot: first, I was prominent in dismantling the barricade; second, I had not been part of the squad who had been poking spike tubing at the "Prison Officers" – they were no longer screws – who had been attempting to persuade the barricading convicts to come out peacefully. He confirmed both points.

"Is it true", I asked, "that a leading light of the tube pokers was the *Torture* Gang Boss Charles Richardson." I put special emphasis on "torture".

The PO looked at me knowingly and replied slowly, "Yes, I believe, according to my officers, that Charles Richardson was part of that group of prisoners." Gordon's eyes flicked cynically over me.

"Is it also true that Charlie Richardson is a notorious gangster who terrorised the London underworld with murder and electric shock torture."

The PO replied to the Chairman, "I believe the prisoner himself would know more about that than I do, sir, but it is true that Charles Richardson is serving twenty-five years for crimes involving torture."

I moved in for the kill.

"Is the officer aware that the torture gang boss exerts the same kind of influence over London prisoners in E-Wing that he did over the London underworld?"

The magistrates were hanging on every word. The PO looked confused. He didn't know what I was driving at or really understand the question. But he, like everyone else, did not like Charlie. He spoke to the Chairman, "We are not aware of Richardson's influence over other prisoners but Richardson is considered…umm…difficult."

"Is the officer aware that I have made numerous complaints to the prison authorities about Richardson terrorising me and requested that I be moved out of his sphere of influence?"

He looked astonished. "Not that I know of."

"But these complaints are documented in my Prison Record."

The magistrates looked expectantly at the PO who now knew, as did Gordon, what my game was. But the magistrates did not have clue. He looked at Gordon who had decided to stay out of the whole business. He was staring into space.

"Well, I am not aware…" the PO faltered, "of such allegations…but…err…" Again he looked for guidance to Gordon who was still staring into space but also shaking his head slightly in exasperation.

Gordon suddenly leaned towards the Chairman and said, "McVicar knows full well that the mutineers destroyed all the prison records."

I put on my most aghast expression and said to the Chairman, "Is the Governor giving evidence or what?

Isn't this tribunal supposed to observe as far as is practical normal court procedures?"

Gordon's face set in disapproval.

The Chairman replied, "Mr McVicar, the bench is quite capable of disregarding remarks made to assist the court but which may be inadmissible."

This is where I thrive – the labyrinthine arguments of the rules of evidence. "Thank you, Mr Chairman. I would like to add an observation about the purported destruction of records – whatever was destroyed by the mutineers – and I wish to emphasise that I was neither a party to that enterprise nor did I destroy any government property. My point is that whatever records were destroyed there are ample copies of the said files. It is well known that I was in fear of my life in E-Wing because of the presence of Charles Richardson and other members of his torture gang..." I wittered on like this until the Chairman indicated that he had heard enough.

There was a hurried consultation between the three of them and he asked, "Does the prisoner wish to examine any more witnesses or testify himself?"

"Thank you, your honour. I do not want to cross-examine any more Prison Officers nor call any witnesses on my behalf but I would request a short adjournment to compose my address to the bench before you deliberate on your verdict."

The three local, middle-aged, male worthies looked like I had just spoken in Ancient Greek or something. They had never heard anything like it. But they gave me fifteen minutes to compose my speech, which I did on paper with bullet points. I then came back in and made a twenty minute speech that had Gordon climbing up his own prison wall.

"I have been in terror of my life because of Charles Richardson ever since I arrived at E-Wing. Even in prison, he and his gang with Mad Frankie Fraser as the enforcer rule London with a rod of iron. My wife and small children (at the time I didn't even have a girlfriend never mind a wife and family) are very precious to me and when the riot was proposed, and I asked not to take part, Richardson reminded me of what could happen to my three-year-old girl…(in a moment of inspiration I named her after my then favourite film star) Angie. I had no choice but to obey Richardson but I was terrified and my will to resist was sapped…" I went on and on like this. I also think I deserve some credit for resisting giving a little sob when I mentioned Angie.

It was one of my finest moments in court and I am still rather proud of my performance. Clearly the bench were impressed because, despite finding me guilty of mutiny, they acquitted me of destroying government property. I also wasted two hours of everyone's time for something that would normally take two minutes.

When I got back in my cell, I shouted out of the window to Charlie who was roughly underneath me, "Chas, I got a guilty on the mutiny but a not guilty on destroying property."

He said, "I don't know how you and Terry do it mate. I really don't. How come?"

"I blamed you Charlie. I said it was all your doing. And they believed – well, half believed me."

"Yeah, yeah. Pull the other one."

Apart from Terry, we all got forty-two days behind our doors and loss of earnings for the same period. My not guilty on destroying government property was rewarded with losing less pay than the others. We also retained all our cell privileges such as radio, tobacco, personal property and there was none of the usual nonsense about putting out our bedding during the day. The mildness of the penalties was almost a vindication of our protest. This was five-star *chokey* (punishment – the expression harks back to the days of bread and water).

Chapter 4
The hunger strike

The leniency shown us inflamed the screws. Instead of E-Wing being a special wing we were special prisoners. They retaliated with the perennial stand-by – *security*. In prison the writ of security is nonpareil. On this occasion it ruled that it was too dangerous to let out more than three prisoners at a time, so they made that an order at slopping out and collecting meals. This meant that the procedure of unlocking, going down to the Ones and collecting food from the hot-plate dragged on for ages. Most of us got dried-out, lukewarm food. To make sure that we got the message, when we had our hour's exercise out on the yard they let us out five at a time.

For me it was a case of beggars not being choosers. Prison food is bad enough as it is, so whether it was cold or hot made little difference to me. There were books to be read, the radio to listen to and, if I needed someone to talk to, I could chat to whoever was in range of my cell window. It was annoying to be upstaged by the screws, but considering what we had got up to it was small beer. Six weeks behind my door was not even a token punishment! However, other people on the wing were incensed at the way the screws were playing their "three prisoners at a time" game. The problem was that the riot and its nominal sanction had also gone to some of the cons' heads. They were not just in a special wing, they were special.

Les decided that he would go on hunger strike in protest at the screws' tactics. To earn the right to be starved in prison – be put on bread and water – I can do all sorts of wonderful things like clump screws, smash prison property, make a pest of myself generally. To starve myself voluntarily is simply wasting my only seed corn. This passion convicts have for starving themselves I have always regarded as a form of self mutilation. How can convicts take the high moral ground? As for us! We were a bunch of murderers, armed robbers and torturers!

Nonetheless, one out, all out – I was on hunger strike. This certainly lifted the spirits of the Geordie screws. There was a sparkle back in their eyes, a cheerful jingle to their keys, their wives and boyfriends could never have been so well serviced. Sometimes when they opened my door for mealtimes and I said "Refuse", they'd stand there savouring the sheer delight of the situation. For about three days I didn't really mind – self-control is good for the soul – and when that began to pall I consoled myself by thinking about the longevity of rats who are starved one day out of three. By the fourth day no rationalisation could compete with the hunger pains.

I went with the madness for another two days, then I mounted a propaganda campaign to persuade everyone to come off. But we had committed ourselves to taking action over the cold-food wheeze and I had to propose an alternative to win hearts and minds. I couldn't ask people just to start eating. The immediate alternative was a dirty protest – shitting up screws. You save it up in a pot, then come out and dump it over a warder.

This is a traditional proactive style of protest that cons like Mad Frankie Fraser turned into a performance art. He would actually find some especially rich food to eat, then he would tweak the consistency of the output with urine and come marching out of his cell holding his pot like a bouquet of flowers. The screws would take off like startled rabbits and Frank would be chasing them all over the wing until he either caught one or the Chief Officer ordered them to subdue him. Whatever way, Frank would get one.

Some of the cons wanted to do this instead of the hunger strike. Perhaps "wanted" is not the right word – they *desired* it. They were back in the chapel again. All very unhealthy. I just wanted to eat but I was trapped in the collective action and couldn't eat without being condemned forever on the prison grapevine as a rat. I had to tout this as an alternative but for sure I was going to be last on the action rota. To talk to everyone I had to go round the cells and talk through the doors; it was like trying to juggle the proverbial mercury balls as no one would come off unless everyone did. The democratic order of the office protest had dissolved into the unanimity rule by which any individual could blackmail the rest to stand by him. There were the usual diehards, but no one more staunch than Charlie.

On the evening of the sixth day, after a blitz of cell-door politicking I got a provisional yes from everyone except Charlie. I left him to last, hoping that faced with a united front not even Charlie would shame the diehards. It was delicately poised as once the diehards reneged, I knew the waiverers would swing back into line.

As I reached his door he was up at his window. "Bill! Bernie! Tony!" he shouted. I heard them answering as I was frantically calling him to come to his door. He bellowed, "You staunch up there? Not weakening, are you? We won't let those Geordie cunts do us." In a parody of loyalty they chorused back exactly the opposite of what they'd just told me.

"Good, we'll show 'em they can't beat us!"

Charlie was a propagandist in his own right. He came over to the door.

"That you, John?"

"As if you didn't know, Chas. You've just undone an hour's work in two seconds."

I gave up then and passively became a starver.

A couple of days later, Dennis Stafford told me what Charlie had been up to. He'd had a visit at the same time as Charlie. One of Charlie's women was visiting him and Dennis had watched her get out some sandwiches and say to him, "Now you eat these." Charlie replied, "No. I can't – I'm on hunger strike."

"Come on."

"No, I can't."

"You're going to, otherwise I will force them down your throat. You just tell the others I have been force feeding you." And then Charlie wolfed down the lot. Dennis discovered from the visit screw that this was the third such visit since the hunger strike began. Dennis, like me, was a Charlie watcher. I know anthropologists would disagree with me but Charlie is far more fascinating than some Borneo tribe untouched by civilisation. He has enjoyed more than his share of what civilisation has to offer and *still* been untouched by it.

Nevertheless, the strike had its compensations. All

the top security risks were housed in cells that had a network of alarm wires embedded in the plaster and connected to the control office. Anyone attempting to dig out set off a warning system. All these cells were on the Twos and Threes on just one side of the wing, which overlooked a busy prison pathway. We would clamber on our cell table and talk out of the cell window. One particular compensation started when Roy Hall was up at his window and amusing himself by hurling volleys of abuse at some screw walking by the wing.

The screw stopped and shouted in his best official snarl, "Get down from that window. **NOW**!" It must have been otherwise quiet because most of us on this side heard it and our response was massive, instant and concerted. It really was the lunatic asylum. Fourteen rabid, starving maniacs frothing at the mouth in our eagerness to pour abuse upon this poor screw. It must have been heard in Durham Town.

The screw's mouth dropped open at this subversion of his universe and suddenly he must have thought that he'd get into trouble for setting us off. He looked round quickly, then just scuttled away. For a couple of days, this was our day's sport. Everyone who passed the wing got the treatment. Gordon, who tended to stand on his dignity, had one dose and we never saw him again. But the doctor got it, the priest and any screw.

Roy also had some fun with the work parties from the main prison that marched past in military style. Instead of abusing them, he'd suddenly shout out an order like "Aboooot turn." The work party would turn round and begin marching the other way. The screw would order them to turn around. Roy would shout something else and the whole exercise would disintegrate into chaos. They had to re-route the work parties, but eventually the staff that had to pass by ignored us and we stopped.

On the eighth day the medics came round and weighed us. I got a shock – I'd lost twenty pounds in body weight! Prime muscle sculpted with weight training sacrificed on the altar of Charlie's fantasies. I genuinely was gutted as it was a lot of weight to lose on just an eight-day crash diet. I lost more than anyone else. I guess my metabolism had gone into overdrive rather than slowed down.

There was no point in arguing with the starvers. Fasting is quite odd. After about five days the hunger pains stop, and though you feel a bit depressed, even that comes and goes. Some of the cons who after four or five days were screaming to call off the strike were now after eight days completely convinced of the justice of their cause and the value of what they were doing. It was almost a form of hysteria.

By now I had learnt that it was futile to argue or reason with Charlie. I had come to realise that only Charlie can change Charlie's mind, but sometimes I would scorn his propaganda broadcasts that he made out the window to keep the troops' spirits up. "We're doing ourselves a lot of good, John. All this publicity is getting us a lot of sympathy."

"No, it's not Chas. Maybe *The Guardian*, but the rest of the papers and the general public think, 'Keep up the good work.'"

"No. You'll see," he'd say.

It is always bad to try to be rational with the irrational as it only makes them worse but Charlie was not so much irrational as perverse. Although he was getting some food – certainly a lot more than me –

whatever was missing from his diet seemed to have affected his brain chemistry. He kept banging on about "conjugals". It became his catchword.

"Any day, we'll have another prisoner director up from the Home Office. And this time we hold out for conjugal visits. It's barbaric not letting a man have sex with his wife. I'm telling you, the country's ready for it..." I don't think Charlie was even married at the time, but I didn't say anything. He was barking up his own tree.

The shock of losing all my prestigious muscles, though, made me decide to eat; but I had to devise a way to do it that would cover up my weakness. Like the first starver, I acted unilaterally. I decided to have a tear-up, but first I went round to each of the six diehards and told them through the cell door, "I am going to eat tonight at tea-time, and tomorrow morning at breakfast I am going to perform. You're one of the starvers who think it's great not eating, but I hope you'll follow me in and join me when I perform, because I've followed you for eight days."

This pre-empted them from pointing the finger of scorn at me: none condemned me outright or said anything insulting. But I was a hostage to my commitment. If I didn't perform as I'd promised I'd be a toe-rag for ever more.

That night I ate my teatime meal and so did about four others who'd got sick of being in the thrall of the diehards. The next morning, I went down to get my breakfast. There were about five screws lounging about the hotplate. I waited until the other two cons who had been unlocked with me had gone back to their cells, then I tipped up the hotplate at the screws, throwing the food all over the place and scattering them. I then went at the previous day's food which had to be kept in the wing and threw that everywhere, urns of tea, custard and trays of food. A screw rushed to grab me, saw he had no help and backed off. I was up for the rugby scrum, which once they rushed me, I knew would take me down.

The whole landing was awash with custard, tea, porridge, soup. Someone must have rung the alarm bell, because by the time I had finished there were about fifteen screws in the middle of the wing looking at me across the culinary devastation. Everyone was banging on their doors and shouting. I backed down the end of the wing opposite the strongbox. No one said anything. After about a minute or so a PO came over, stepping gingerly round the mess on the floor. "You try and grab me and I'll break your jaw," I said. I was back in my favourite pose again.

"No, no," he said, holding up his hands. "I'm not going to do anything like that. Are you going away to your cell?"

"Nope. You're going to have to put me in there," I said, pointing to the strongbox (punishment cell) that was at the end of the wing on the Ones.

"You're being silly, you know."

"You know how silly I am," I replied. It wasn't my usual grade of dialogue but perhaps the lack of food and the pressure was taking its toll.

He went back to the other screws; a few of them were fingering the straps of their sticks, raring to go. They had every cause to batter me and they easily could. I was probably not even going to get one good punch in. I thought, *Well, now you're committed, things can only get worse.* But I felt determined and confident. I was there about five minutes. No one said anything.

There was a loose orange near me, left over from two meals back, I picked it up, peeled and ate it.

The PO came back over and said, "Look, Mac, we're not going to put you away. You can stand there till the governor comes in, if you like. It's up to you." He paused, looking at me calmly. "Why don't you go away to your cell?"

I didn't feel quite so brave now and the belting that I was on, loomed up a lot more painfully. I went back to my cell.

Everyone was shouting, "What happened?" I got up at the window and told them. I censored how the fear had got to me and just said I'd come up because I started to feel stupid just standing there. But I ribbed the diehard starvers about what they would be doing. "And what have the starvers done" became my swansong. I committed myself to performing again the next day but I was also aware that the authorities were not going to let E-Wing fester much longer.

Nothing else happened that day, but about eight o'clock that night my door opened and a big craggy-faced Geordie PO, about six foot three inches, 220 pounds, stepped in. He was built for trouble and he had the attitude for it, too.

"Pack your kit McVicar, we're moving you over to the other side." That meant they were taking me to the main prison.

I replied cockily, "Wanna bet, sweetheart? No one's moving me over to the other side."

"McVicar," he said wearily, "you cannie do nought about it. You're going to be moved. Whatever way you go, you are going. I've got orders to move you, with whatever force is required. There's a doctor and a magistrate outside to witness it."

He was a big hard bastard who'd seen the tearaways come and go, but never past him. He had the confidence to know that they could have the first strike and that it would be their last.

He moved out of the doorway. There was a smug little man standing by the railings, he was the magistrate. There were screws everywhere. I couldn't see the doctor but I had already decided that the way to handle this was to make sure I didn't have to see him. This was one you held your hands up to.

"Why just me?"

"Don't worry. Some of the others will be going as well."

Going was the operative word. I took counsel from TINA – there is no alternative. But, of course, there always are alternatives. Funk, though, makes exactly the kind of blinkers you need to screen them off.

"All right, then. I ain't got much choice, have I?"

"No, you ain't, have you?" the Geordie screw said in his best cockney, a half-smile on his face. He read me.

I put my odds and ends into a pillow case, then walked out of the cell. The screws packed themselves around me and I didn't think it wise to try to stop at someone's cell to tell them what had happened. While I didn't like caving in, I had got what I wanted – I could now eat without any other con being able to finger me as a rat.

I was escorted over to a strongbox in the main prison. Four others followed me, including Charlie, I later found out. The next morning I was parked in a cell on the bottom landing of the main prison. Charlie fell on his feet as he got transferred to Parkhurst special wing, which in terms of conditions was the best of the wings. I settled down to read and make the best of it.

I never spoke to anyone and never saw anyone I knew. I paced up and down on a patch of ground near the hospital for half an hour in the morning and half an hour in the afternoon. It was spring and there was some grass and some flower beds outside the hospital. I used to get quite sentimental over this little bit of the outside.

I was a star attraction to the Geordie cons: they used to line up outside my door before going off to work and invariably someone would clock my cell card, which was on a clipboard on the wall adjoining one's cell.

"Cor, twenty-three years, what can he dun to get that?"

"I'd top meself. I really would. I couldna do it."

"He dunna look any different from anyone else."

Sometimes when the screws slopped me out late I'd have an audience. The short-termers would look at me like I was some freak of nature. I suppose to them I was – I had a throw-away-the-key sentence, I wore no shoes or tie and no screw bawled me out. I had some kind of dignity. Well, in my own head, I guess.

After about a week of this another running battle developed over the original cause of all the trouble: prison clothing. I'd come over in just my trainers, overalls, shirt, vest, pants and socks. Every now and then, some screws would open the door and casually try to tick off what I had against a clothing list. It was "back in the army" time again.

"Just a stock check, McVicar. Have you got a tie, shoes..." Shoes! I was allergic to the word!

"Look, pal, don't come in here with silly little lists. I've got exactly what I want. And I don't want ties and shoes, and I am not having ties and shoes."

"I'm only doing ma job, checking what you've got."

"Yeah, I know." I gave him a lecture on the facts of 23 years. "Look I am on 23 years and I have already lost most of my remission. I am locked up 23 hours a day. I don't bother anyone – don't bother me. 'Cos I ain't wearing shoes, ties, or greys (prison issue flannel trousers and jacket) and I ain't going to. Alright?"

This worked for a while but after about a fortnight someone thought up a way to outflank me. In a local prison such as Durham, prisoners who are designated escape risks have to pile their clothing, knife, fork and spoon on their chair and place it on the landing outside their cell overnight. It is standard procedure and ever since I had been grounded in the main prison that is what I did. One morning the door opened, my chair was quickly put inside the cell and the door quickly shut.

Screws don't do anything at speed unless it is something prisoners don't like. I got up with an ominous feeling. On the top of the chair seat was the trouble – a shiny black pair of prison issue shoes and no trainers. In a fury, I grabbed them and stuffed them out of the window, then waited to get unlocked. They let me stew for some time, but eventually I came out in my bare feet to slop out (go to the recess). The screw whom I fancied was responsible was standing by the recess.

"Take my trainers, did yer?"

"No, I never took them; didn't know you even had any." He was looking very warily at the chamber pot. Without my record they had no means of knowing whether I was in the Mad Frankie Fraser camp.

"You fucking took them, you cunt," I snarled.

"Not me, honest." He was still wary of the unemptied pot.

I had made him frightened enough to lie. It was about all I was going to get to salve my bruised ego. Really, what I wanted to do was clump him, but you can't do what you want to do in prison. If you try to, you lose. Big time. You can't win in prison: the best you can do is never give in, never concede defeat, even when you know you can't win.

The next time I came out of my cell the dreaded shoes were outside on the landing again. I picked them up contemptuously and flung them right down the wing watching them slide some thirty yards along the polished tiles. I was still in bare feet. Of course, even I was aware of how absurd the whole schemozle was but that couldn't help me step out of it. I was in prison and this is what prisons are like – mindless, rule-mongering, pettifogging institutions. Screws set up the game and you have to play against them or become like them.

As I came out of the recess, a decent sort of screw who had worked in E-Wing came up to me. "What are you walking about like that for, Mac?" he asked.

"They nicked my trainers off my chair last night and I can't wear shoes." I shrugged and grimaced at the idiocy of it all.

"Well, we can't have you walking about like that. I'll get you a pair of slippers. What size do you take?'"

"Sevens. Thanks. Thanks a lot." I think I meant it. I was feeling persecuted and sorry for myself; I felt inordinately grateful to be on the end of a friendly gesture. About an hour and a half later, he opened my door and gave me a pair of cell slippers. I was so grateful – not because I couldn't walk about in bare feet – but because he had crossed the line for me. Later when I got back to the special wing, someone ran this screw down and I wouldn't have it at any price.

But the game played on. Gordon made wearing shoes a condition of my being allowed exercise, so I stayed in my kennel all day. When Gordon came round on his daily pit stop to see those on punishment, I accused him of being vindictive and abusing his authority. He ignored my indictment. I didn't swear or curse him, just tried to shame him. I really missed the grass and the flower beds. They reminded me of the outside and my mum who loved flowers. Even people like me get sentimental when they hit rock bottom.

About a week later, a screw opened my door and said, "The Home Secretary wants to see you in a minute." I knew it wasn't a joke as screws don't have the imagination to be that surreal. I hadn't shaved for about four days. The spit-'n'-polish lot like everyone to shave every morning, so I didn't very often. My hair was cropped in a convict cut – it was shorter than my facial stubble. I ran a brush over it nevertheless. I thought I ought to make some kind of show for the Home Secretary. Even the haircut was a symbol of contempt for authority.

In the old days, hair was shaven to counter lice but the in-the-army mentality likes the short back and sides. They like to think of their "inmates" – another one of their euphemisms – being rehabilitated by army training. Rehabilitation was another one of their terms to warp the reality of prison. I would never pretend to be an inmate who was undergoing rehabilitation. I was a convict and my shaven head was an intrusive symbol of the reality of prison not the ideological façade that the prison authorities use to hide it. I was also aware that even in debunking the system I was still being defined by it.

I was chuffed at being singled out by Home Secretary James Callaghan. I assumed that it was because of the petition that I'd written, which though it did not bear my signature was written in my handwriting. There was probably only three or so possible candidates for authorship. My work had reached the eyes of the Home Secretary and he was interested in meeting the author! It was all grist to my mill that I had Oscar Wilde potential.

About fifteen minutes later, the same screw opened my cell door and I followed him with my slippers flapping on the tiles. We walked to a nearby small office, the screw opened the door and I stepped inside. James Callaghan was facing the doorway sitting on a chair behind a small plastic-topped table. Gordon was seated primly in a corner by himself, legs crossed and arms folded across his chest. The Chief Officer was standing to my right by the door. Gordon spoke as I stood before the desk. "The Home Secretary is visiting Durham and he has decided to see you." As with his body language, so with his intonation: I was another piece of livestock that he and his kind were paid to keep in our pens.

"Thank you, thank you," I addressed Callaghan not Gordon.

"Sit down McVicar, sit down," Callaghan said. The chief pushed a chair to me and I sat on it. Callaghan is a big, open man with a genial look. He said invitingly, "Is there anything that you would like to talk to me about?"

"Well yes, Mr Callaghan, I certainly would."

"Well, that's what I'm here for. You can say what

you like. No one will stop you." Obviously no one had told him that I was a classic barrack-room agitator who could not even shut himself up. But he gave me an encouraging grin. He was relaxed and looked like he was enjoying himself, although I couldn't think why.

I went into our side of the dispute, but played it very low key. I emphasised the non-violence of our protest and stressed the corner the governor had forced us into. I pointed out how the Home Office's own council for penal reform had recommended for the chop many of the regulations that the Governor was bent on enforcing. Actually re-enforce as they had already lapsed under the previous governor.

I was on song and Callaghan seemed to enjoy the rhetoric rather than the argument. He never argued the toss; indeed, he did not even interrupt. And I felt that his unvoiced opinion was that Gordon had pushed his genuine discretion over such rules into provocative territory that events had shown he could not defend. But I knew he wasn't about to sell out Gordon. Nor could I believe he was interested in debating the merits of the mutiny. I suppose he was looking at the monkeys in the zoo that he had overall responsibility for, which was why he listened.

When I had finished, he began, "I stand by the Governor."

I interjected a quick "Of course."

"This situation is in some respects similar to an industrial dispute, where both sides have dug in, and stubbornness is only making it worse. But the governor was perfectly within his rights in issuing those orders. I and my department back him up to the hilt. On the other hand, I don't want to lock you chaps up like this, but what alternative is there when you carry on as you do? Everyone gets on to me and you don't give us any choice but to crack down. You can't expect to be treated responsibly when you behave like this."

It was not appropriate to gainsay him and I didn't. I said crisply, "I know." I was feeling that he had given me as much as I could expect, and he was a busy man and I wasn't. It was time to dismiss myself.

But he encouraged me to talk about prisons generally. I felt like I wasn't being treated like a prisoner but an equal whose views he wanted. I made some comments about the special wings and the frustrations they involved. He referred to the dispersal policy and I argued the advantages of a top-security jail. He rejected this. It was like a discussion but emotionally I kept wavering between feeling flattered and that, as I had said what I had to say, I should get back where I belonged – in my kennel.

Then, as my audience was tailing off, he asked "Tell me, what do you do all day"

"I stay in my cell and read," I replied.

"What, all day?" He looked surprised, but sceptical as if I was exaggerating.

"Yes." I decided that it was too good an opportunity to miss having a pop at Gordon. I added, "The Governor won't let me go out on exercise because I won't wear prison shoes." I wasn't hustling for sympathy – I just said it as a matter of fact.

He looked slightly sad but also resigned. I suppose he had seen the same kind of petty self-destructiveness in numerous industrial disputes. I stood up to leave. I was on my best behaviour.

"I don't want to waste any more of your time, Mr Callaghan. Thank you for listening to me."

Of course, I had scored a point but it had come out

in context; Gordon bit, though. He couldn't let me even win a fair point in open play.

"Wait a moment, McVicar. Tell the Home Secretary why you threw the new shoes you were issued with out of the window and why you're not allowed on exercise." He was the dog with the bone.

I looked at him like he was the blinkered protester. Inside I could feel that warm glow, when you draw the hand that can't lose. He'd shopped himself in front of the Home Secretary. I was still standing and looking at him, then I delivered one of my best one-liners: "I don't suppose the Home Secretary wants to hear about my shoes, Governor."

There was venom in his eyes; contempt in mine. This was what it was really about: a petty conflict in which both sides had lost not only all sense of proportion but also humour.

"What's all this about, then?" asked Callaghan, picking up on the hidden agenda.

Gordon could not leave it alone. "Mr Home Secretary, McVicar was issued with a new pair of shoes. It's because he threw them out of the window and refuses to wear them, that he cannot go out on exercise."

Callaghan was looking from him to me. He was intrigued by the shoes.

"Well, come on McVicar, tell me about the shoes." He was openly amused. And I wasn't about to look a gift horse in the mouth. I already had my line.

I sat down again. "He's just to trying to give a bad impression of me, Mr Home Secretary." I had picked up on the official form of address from Gordon – it was the only thing I ever learned from him.

"I came over here from E-Wing in a pair of

trainers, which I wore for a few weeks. No one objected. Then about a week ago a warder pinched them off my chair. Every night, over here, I have to put my clothing out on a chair; it's an escape precaution and it's returned to me in the morning. This particular morning the trainers were gone and a pair of shoes had been put in their place. I admit I stuffed them out of the window. I was angry and annoyed. But these people are supposed to be setting us an example. They shouldn't stoop to our kind of tactics in order to get their way. That only confirms us in our behaviour."

Callaghan thought all this highly amusing and turned to Gordon, "Were the trainers pinched off his chair?" Inside Gordon must have been squirming but rather than risk sinking deeper into the mire he passed the buck to the Chief Officer.

The chief took his cue from Callaghan. He was smiling a bit – reluctantly, but still smiling. "Well, yes, they were taken off his chair. On my orders because I knew he wouldn't give them up if he was asked."

This was true, of course, but no one knew it was. And I wasn't going to let it invalidate my argument.

"That's not the point. It's for the authorities always to do things correctly. It's our prerogative to get up to tricks like that, not the authorities."

Callaghan broke up the backbiting.

"McVicar, I'm not in the habit of asking for personal favours, but will you do something for me?"

"Yes, of course." It was obvious what was coming.

"Will you wear your shoes if they are given back to you?"

"Yes, certainly, of course, I will." I was falling over myself to please.

"Then, I'm sure, the Governor will let you go out

on exercise," he said, turning to Gordon and smiling broadly.

Gordon wasn't going to see the joke, though – he didn't fraternise with the livestock. His face set grimly as he replied pedantically, "Yes, if he wears the shoes, he can go out on exercise."

Then Callaghan asked me a few questions about where I came from and things like that. I guess he was wondering why I had thrown away my life to the prison system. He was a good guy. I always warm to him when I see him on TV.

I went back to my cell. A screw gave me the shoes. They had lost their symbolism – they didn't matter now. I put them on and went out on exercise that afternoon. Flowers and grass by the prison hospital, but always the prison wall over-shadowing everything. Callaghan was the titular head of the system but he wasn't of it. He reminded me of the outside – I guess because he was normal.

As a rule, prisons bring out the worst in people – whether it is staff or inmates it is just the same. That is not to say that society can dispense with prisons – they are an indispensable, necessary evil. But you can see their unhealthy nature in those who are attracted to campaigns or organisations aimed at changing them. Whether they want to make them easier or harder, these people are as sick as what they want to change.

Being touched by the outside made me nostalgic for my home life. I thought of the park opposite where I'd take my niece and our dog for a walk. A six-year-old chirping and chirruping beside me, demanding "swingies" and "carries" and always getting them. Throwing Max's ball and chasing him when he brought it back to get it out of his mouth. Stopping at the swings and tying Max to the railings as she swung backwards and forwards. When he barked, her saying, "Isn't he a naughty boy, John? We'll leave him at home tomorrow."

And all my tomorrows would be spent like today – regretting the past and dying in the future. Maybe in twenty years I would be released as sick and twisted as I was already becoming. How could I even hope, never mind imagine, that within six months I would be free?

Chapter 5
The hell-hole cools down

I was given some more bang-up for my display round the hotplate, then about seven weeks later, as my punishment was coming to an end, Assistant Governor Greene came over to see me and told me that I would be going back to E-Wing. I wasn't happy with the news. Hadn't I caused enough trouble to be moved?

Most of the other cons had been transferred. Greene assured me that things would be different but I wasn't listening. I had been isolated for a long time and I had retreated into books and myself. I didn't want to return to what I already knew...but a few weeks later I was returned to E-Wing.

Roy Hall met me. I was a bit grumpy, looking for something to find fault with. "John, it's different gravy now. You'll see. We have got it all our own way. The screws are off our back and Charlie is in Parkhurst. OK, we are still in the dog-kennel but we don't have to beg for our supper..." He convinced me.

When we were filling in our stories of what had happened to each of us, I told him about Callaghan coming over to see me and how he had especially asked to talk to me. I was preening with this confirmation of my importance. Roy pricked my bubble, "He saw four of us, John. And I said don't forget to see the others in the main prison. He said he would and I suggested your name."

Everything really was different in E-Wing.

Gordon had relinquished all control to Greene who was now effectively the controller of our privileges and conditions. A new exercise yard had been finished, big enough to play football in; there was also an indoor yard that was floodlit; the wrought-iron shop was due to open in a week's time; the regime was now structured so that we had complete freedom in the wing. We were unlocked at seven in the morning and did not have to return to our cells until nine in the evening. We ate all our meals on association and, within the limits prescribed, we arranged our lives without any interference from the screws. There was strictly no ordering about just for the sake of it. Not that there had been much before but it suited us to remember it as if there was.

There were seven normal cons who had the run of the bottom three landings. The top landing was for the sex cases – there were now four monsters up there but they had their own facilities in a self-contained unit. They might as well have been in a different prison.

I palled up with Roy and, with the ironmongery shop soon opening, we both decided we'd be wing cleaners. Neither of us fancied the idea of making things out of wrought iron. It sounded a bit too much like work. And we'd been sent to prison for punishment, not work.

Previously the cleaning had been done by cons brought over from the main prison but now it was hardly done at all. The wing was dirty and we decided to make a job of it. The screws were surprised to see us on our hands and knees but their faces turned quite respectful when they saw the way we attacked it. We had two catwalk landings to clean – Twos and Threes – with their TV rooms and recesses. The Ones' landing was plastic tiled and had a recess coming off together with a shower room and a kitchen, which was just a converted cell with a sink for washing up and a stove for cooking.

We grafted like Spanish donkeys…for two hours in the morning with sweat coursing down our face, then laid about for the rest of the day. We worked unsupervised and set our own standards; the landings and recesses were spotless, so no one could or did complain.

Roy and I took stock of the new exercise yard and badgered Greene to let us buy some tennis rackets and balls. He went one better and bought them out of prison funds. We marked up a court in the yard and we had a net made up in the prison workshop. We used a couple of weight-lifting stands as net stanchions. We also had a new inside yard that was walled in by the inside L of the wing, the wall of the wrought-iron shop. This was covered by translucent Perspex and was floodlit. We applied the same lobbying we had used in creating a tennis court to make a badminton court in this yard.

The tennis and badminton courts tended to be used during the exercise periods in the morning and the afternoon. Our other sporting facility, weight-lifting, tended to be an evening activity. While Roy and I cleaned, the other five worked in the shop on the weekdays for a few hours in the morning and in the evening after the exercise periods. After some time we had a couple of lecturers a week in the evenings, one of whom was Laurie Taylor who inspired me to start reading sociologists like Erving Goffman. Then we got cooking lessons, which was just an excuse to cook a decent meal twice a week. We still had the two TV rooms on the Twos and Threes and the piped radio in the cells. As prisons go it was a rose garden without, as yet, any thorns.

Charlie had been 'ghost-trained' down to Parkhurst the morning after I'd been transferred to the main prison. Their wing was even better than ours now as they had a garden and grew loads of vegetables and at one time had a few marijuana plants. Charlie, however, was still obsessed with conjugals and when he saw that they were not on at Parkhurst he started agitating the other cons, telling them that in the wing at Durham we had an arrangement with the screws to leave us alone in the visiting room when our wives or girlfriends visited us. That nearly led to a riot and the authorities decided to send him back to Durham.

Anyway, two months into our 5-star conversion of the hell-hole, Greene came up to Roy and me while we were making tea after our cleaning stint. An ex-navy officer, Greene was untouched by the prison system. He was a decent, modest, solid Englishman who didn't have a vindictive bone in his body or a sly thought in his head. "Good morning gentlemen. Everything OK?"

We always addressed him as "Mr Greene" and we had a bantering easy-going relationship with him; yet I for one never really saw him as a prison official. He just was too nice a man to be working in prison.

"Hall," he said to Roy, "how would you like it if your friend Charlie Richardson was to come back here?"

Roy looked startled, "Charlie's coming back! What's happened at Parkhurst then? What's he been up to?"

Greene smiled, "It is not official yet but I think you might be in for a surprise."

"What's he done then, Mr Greene? There'll be a

reason. There always is with Charlie." He looked mischievously at Greene.

Greene could not resist conceding that there had been problems, "Well, as you know, his experiences here rather turned him into a firebrand and after some local difficulties I believe the authorities decided it would be better for all concerned if he came back here."

We went up to the TV room to drink our tea and watch the midday news. I was rather pleased that Charlie was coming as for all his deviousness at least he was a colourful character. The denizens of prisondom tend to be a pretty drab lot. Roy shook his head at me, "No John, you don't know Charlie. He'll be a pest. We've got it nice and sweet here now but he'll never be satisfied. Whatever Charlie gets he wants more. That's the way he is."

Charlie duly arrived, scowling at being back in Durham. We all greeted him as he came through the gate. He was all smiles and handshakes; Charlie is a charmer when he wants to be. Within a couple of days, though, he showed his true colours. When he was told that he was to be transferred back to Durham, he'd organised a visit for the next day. It was one of his many girlfriends but when he went into our visiting room he discovered that there was a six inch piece of Perspex across the visiting table. This was one of the few remnants of Gordon's regime.

It didn't bother me as I rarely had a visit but, as none of the other wings had it, Roy and I had raised it with Greene. He had told us to leave it with him and not to raise it with Gordon. In fact, we never spoke to Gordon, who rarely came into the wing anyway.

But after he had finished his visit Charlie went on

On the set of the film *McVicar*, John McVicar, Steven Berkov, Roger Daltrey, and Wally Probyn. *1980*

and on about the Perspex.

'They ain't got it on the *island* (Parkhurst) It's a liberty. What we going to do about it?"

Roy attempted to placate him, "'Charlie, we know. Greene's looking into it. Give him time."

"Look, they're taking you for mugs. This is saying we are second-class citizens. It's outrageous. I'm going to see that fucking Governor."

I always thought we were convicts and, while I could entertain 'prisoners' and understand 'inmates', I had never considered 'citizens'. I didn't see the point of telling him that imprisonment actually is the forfeiture of citizenship. I was also baffled why he was so irate about the bit of Perspex, but I knew he wouldn't get any joy from Gordon.

I said, "You'll draw a blank and that will louse it up

for Greene. None of us have spoken to Gordon since the trouble. He'll be de-*lighted* to blank you."

"John, it's a liberty, and he's in the wrong. How do you know Greene's not kidding you? What you think he is on your side? All he is really is just another fucking screw."

I looked at Roy in resignation. You can't argue with Charlie. He made a governor's application, went in and laid the law down to Gordon and got a blank. Eventually the Perspex went, but it stayed there the longer because of Charlie. Before it went though, I asked Roy why Charlie had such a bee in his bonnet about it.

"He gets at it John. He gets Eva or Helen or one of 'em to come without their bra and knickers on and he has a grope. You've never seen him in the visiting room. Honestly, if my wife and kids are up, it's embarrassing. But you know what he's like."

There were a few more transfers but by June the wing had stabilised around the seven people who were there when I escaped. I was now twenty-eight years old and serving twenty-three years for offences relating to armed robbery. I was only four years into my sentence and I didn't even think of a release date. I was mousey-haired, 5' 9" and 12 stone; very fit and because of weightlifting a bit bodybuilder muscular. But I was already a recluse, cynical, pessimistic and more than a bit of a moaner.

Roy complemented me in some ways as he was gregarious, optimistic and invariably cheerful. We worked out together and played tennis and badminton against each other. He was 26, blonde, stocky, short and weighed around eleven stone. He was serving 10 years for his involvement in Charlie's torture gang.

Unlike most of us, Roy could see the end of his sentence.

There was Charlie, of course. He was on 25 years and only two years into it. Thirty-four: about 5' 8" inches, 168 pounds, short legs with a stocky frame, blond thinning hair and a thin delicately broken nose. A broad face, confident and calculating in repose, but when he laughed or smiled it showed an infectious humour and sparkle. Charlie had more than lived, he'd lived it up. He hated being in prison as much as anyone but in a slightly different way than, say, me. What killed Charlie was being cut off from all that he enjoyed outside; whereas for me, while that also figured, it was more the humiliation of being controlled and, in a sense, farmed, by other men.

Charlie was a good judge of human nature, especially its weaknesses. He once said to me, "You know the way I judge people John? It's in how much out of hundred quid I'd lend them. That's how I reckon someone."

"How much would you lend me Charlie?" I asked. I laughed to make it easy for him to insult me.

"You mate? Well, you know…it wouldn't be much. You'd probably be back in prison before you could pay me back."

Charlie was different. A lot of cons will make all manner of claims to boost their status or reputation. But I never heard Charlie tell a story, whether true or false, for that purpose. He didn't care what others thought of him unless it blocked him off from something he wanted. I always knew when I spoke to Charlie that there was far more going on in his mind that he couldn't come clean about – and didn't – than with most people.

Adam Faith, who played Wally Probyn,
on the set of *McVicar*

Wally Probyn was another Londoner who like me had served a lot of time. In fact, Wally was what the Americans call a "state-reared youth". He had spent much of his life in penal institutions and fought them by escaping. He was hipped on escape; it was really a prison career. Plotting to escape and sometimes achieving it was his life. He was a nightmare for the prison authorities to contain. They had put him in Dartmoor when he was in his teens, where he became gay for a while. Wally was placid and less aggressive than most criminals: an appeaser by nature, but he would sulk and become vague and remote if annoyed by anything.

He was 34, curly dark hair, average height with a bodybuilder's physique. The last time he had been arrested for firing at a detective, he was beaten to a pulp and they broke about ten bones. He still got 12 years in 1985. He had metal pins everywhere, so it was a miracle that he was able-bodied.

Wally was very friendly with Tony Dunford who was six years into a double life: he'd stabbed one boy when he was sixteen and killed another teenager while he was in prison. He had been sentenced to death but been reprieved and was still only twenty-one or twenty-two. Tall, about six foot two inches, a stringy but sleek 168 pounds; good-looking, bespectacled, thick black curly hair, smooth, olive skin - faintly Byronic. He was very intelligent – read poetry and the ancient classics – very articulate and, as we were both passionate self-educators, we'd engage in marathon arguments and discussions that the others found totally unintelligible. More often than not he would get the better of me. He would sulk if upset and sometimes withdraw completely to his cell. Not a committed or socialised criminal, and for all the enormity of his offences, probably the least likely to re-offend.

As an adolescent he'd twisted up emotionally and become burdened by the conviction that to be worthy he must be tough and courageous. Yet this was alien to his basic nature and he couldn't cope with the resulting conflict of reconciling what he was and what he aspired to be. The tragedy for him, and for his second victim, was that retribution could only be exacted in an environment which operates on the same machismo that precipitated the first murder. He was probably the only con in the wing who felt guilt for his crimes.

Tony Creamer was a 29-year-old Scot who had killed a man by karate, or so at least he claimed in court. It earned him a life sentence of which he had done two years. If he'd come clean in court about the homosexual element in the murder, he would probably have drawn 5 years for manslaughter. We called him Karate because he knew nothing about the martial art. Aside from not practising Karate, he never even worked-out. He was five foot eight inches, 150 pounds with greasy long black hair. He had no friends. He was transparently disturbed and would become excited and agitated by any mention of sex or any number of other subjects to which he was sensitive. Highly aggressive, but without the capacity or the courage to direct his aggression against the staff or other cons it would translate itself into raving tirades against the screws, the regime, the government, society, the world.

Charlie did not team up with Roy – who still spent a lot of time with me – but he adopted another scrap metal merchant who'd just acquired 14 years over a string of sensational shootings and bomb attacks in the Fulham area. Tony Lawrence, in fact, was a jumped-up mug who had been transformed into a gangster by his own propaganda combined with the compulsion of the authorities to invent hard nuts to fill their special wings. He arrived from Wandsworth Prison where he'd obviously found his level. He was dressed in prison greys, wore a tie and for the first hour was calling our screws "sir". When I saw him, I cringed in embarrassment; when I heard him, I shrivelled up in shame.

He was a thick-set five foot nine inches, 175 pounds man with glasses on a bullet-scarred, beaten-up, moon-shaped face. He rather liked being a special category con and quickly came under Charlie's wing. I don't know if they compared the prices of church roof lead or what but as I kept away from Lawrence as much as possible I never found out. In a normal prison, I would have shunned the likes of him and Karate but the wing was like a little fish bowl where you had to swim with people you'd normally eat.

There was another con who lived on the fringes of our society. This was John Straffen, the child murderer. He had killed a pair of young twin children and had later escaped from Broadmoor and killed another child. He hadn't sexually assaulted any of them. He had a mental age of about seven: he wasn't so much abnormal as subnormal. A shambling bent wreck of a man, who at thirty-eight looked fifty-five or sixty, he had a head like that of an old comic character, the Mekon, whom I used to follow in the *Eagle* when I was a kid. It was bald, bulbous and dome-shaped. He had shifty, evasive eyes and a stuttering, sly speech.

In the Parkhurst special wing, the other cons had allowed him to potter about as he liked, but in E-Wing he was located with the monsters on the Fours. They ostracised him as he wasn't interested in talking about kidnapping and raping children. I suppose they couldn't forgive him for wasting the opportunity he'd had to bugger all that uncut babymeat. It has always puzzled me why these child rapists, even when they've kidnapped a girl, will always go for the arse. There must be a reason but I suppose I'd rather stay ignorant. Anyway as the other three completely ignored him, Straffen would not associate with them, which meant that he was totally isolated.

He was a lonely, tragic figure but I don't think any of us really cared about his predicament. He was adopted by us mainly because of Charlie. We were sitting eating lunch and Charlie said, "You know on the *island* we let Straffen do the washing up and sweep up and that." Roy and I exchanged glances. Charlie continued, "He's harmless, ain't he? I mean it is not as if he knew what he was doing. Probably don't even know he did it."

Wally piped up too. As he had also been at Parkhurst with Straffen, Wally genuinely felt sorry for him. "He's a poor, lost soul. There is no need to see him like he is. We could let him down here. It would be no skin off our noses."

We all said our piece and the only one who opposed the proposal was Karate. He began ranting and raving about letting sex cases mix with us. Tony Dunford explained to him rather like you would teach a child arithmetic that Straffen was not a sex case.

"He strangled three fucking wee kids, if that ain't a sex case, what is?"

Tony replied dryly, "Someone who sexually assaults children, Karate."

"I say he should stay where is. He better not come near me. I'll smash the fucking animal."

After much soul-searching, it was agreed to let him partially mix with us. Roy and I approached Greene and Wally spoke to Straffen. We used the Twos' TV room for eating and watching TV, so we let him use the Threes. We got him working for us too but, as with a small child, it proved easier to do it yourself. He would mop away at the same spot never knowing when it was clean enough to move onto the next one. Things like that. He'd done 22 years already and was a goner. His favourite TV programme was *Watch with Mother*.

Roy and I used to give him porn mags and tease him about his sex life. "You've been wanking Straff, ain't yer?" Roy would say. He'd point his finger at Straffen and narrow his eyes. "I can tell. Now own up. Otherwise we won't let you see *Watch with Mother* today." He'd blush and stammer. We'd invent stories about some film star like Liz Taylor or the Queen and tell him about the games they would get up to. He took everything we said as gospel. It was like we were his older brothers. We selected one attractive woman who worked in the hospital and who walked past the wing twice a day. We gave her a name. "That's Carol, Straff. She's like all nurses – can't get enough. We get Greeney to take us over to the hospital, Straff, and we give her a good seeing to… She loves it."

Sometimes we'd catch him at the window drooling while he waited for Carol to come past. I don't think she would have appreciated what we were up to but it passed the time. Roy and I did a lot of this kind of stuff. It amused us to kid people into making exhibitions of themselves. Lawrence got the full treatment.

He started weightlifting with Charlie and we quickly started to send up his Popeye muscles. Tony was a prime mover, "Fucking hell, Law you're a natural. I never seen someone put on so much muscle so quickly." He invented a competition for *The Over-Thirties Mr Great Britain* that was judged on photographs. We got Lawrence posing in the middle of the room for his photoshoot. We would debate the merits of his different poses for showcasing his muscles. As he was only allowed to send in three snapshots much time had to be spent selecting the right poses. Tony Dunford was the master at this. He'd choreograph some contorted pose, then stand back and whistle loud and long, and say, "God, that shows the arm off beautifully and it certainly is one powerful arm." This one ran and ran until Lawrence made an application to Greene to have the necessary photographs taken to enter the competition.

To avoid hurting his feelings, the ever-diplomatic Greene said he'd look into it. He casually dropped into the Twos' TV room, which was mine and Roy's den during the daytime, and said with a smile, "I suppose the photographs were your idea?"

Roy laughed. "You've captured us bang to rights again, Mr Greene. This one's working so well it's getting embarrassing." Greene couldn't help laughing, but Lawrence was discreetly informed that he couldn't be photographed to enter *The Over-Thirties Mr Great Britain*. Even when we had got bored with it, Lawrence would still pose around asking how his biceps were coming on.

We even managed to pull one on Charlie, which sort of came out of another elaborate send up of Tony. It began over Tony ogling some young woman who every Saturday morning used to show viewers how to sail small boats. For some reason she rang Tony's bell and there he'd be glued to the TV every Saturday morning. We encouraged him to write to her, which he did but funked posting the letter. Roy and I sneaked into his cell, copped the letter, addressed and posted it. He just cringed.

But Charlie picked up on this and told him, "Tony, I know a girl you can write to, Candy. She's a stripper in the West End. Right sort. Tell her you met her with me and Frank (Fraser) one night and I'll bet you she'll write back. With a bit of luck she might even come and see you. On my life, she's a real good girl."

Roy and I took more notice of this than Tony

who was still writhing with embarrassment. But the next day we clued him up to get hold of Charlie and get Candy's address. He then wrote the letter and let Charlie read it before pretending to post it. About a week later, Roy and I dropped it on Charlie. We were sorting out the grub at lunch-time – as usual he was late – but when he arrived Roy said off-handedly, "Tony's got a letter off that Candy and the rat won't let us see it. She's sent him a load of nude photos, too, Chas. They're so strong there's been a steward's (inquiry) about whether he can have them."

Even as he shook his head, Charlie's eyes dilated. "Nahhh…you two are at it."

"No, he's in there now, arguing the toss," I said referring to Tony having to argue his case with the PO.

Charlie nibbled. "Really? What, straight up?"

"There he is. He must have got 'em," I said. Tony had timed it perfectly. He walked along the Twos and into his cell with a big envelope we'd buzzed out of the office under his arm. He put the envelope on his locker and shut the door, even checking the handle to make sure it was locked. Charlie did a double-take.

"I saw the PO looking at them in the office, Chas," Roy said. "It was coming out of his eyes. And to think you put him onto her."

When we were seated round the table eating, Charlie asked Tony whether he had got a letter from Candy. Tony looked up from his grub and just said, "Yeah," then went back to his food.

"Don't we get a look, Tony?" I said plaintively.

"I've already told you. No," Tony replied.

'Nice sort of chap you are," Roy added.

"Roy, do you let me read your letters?" Tony asked in a didactic tone.

"Tony, we don't want to look at the letter, all we want to do is look at the photos," I said. "The screws have seen them, why not us?"

"John, if your *bird* (girlfriend) sent you some nude photos, would you show them to me?"

I replied, "I don't have a *bird* but if she was a stripper I might. Yeah, why not."

As cunning as an old fox, Charlie had nosed what way the wind was blowing and he came right in on Tony's case. "Nah, Tony's right. If he doesn't want to show 'em to you, that's his business."

Tony responded gratefully, "Thanks, Chas."

Charlie got out the grease gun. "I told you son. She's a good girl. She'll visit you if you play your cards right. You keep her sweet, son. You never know what might come of it."

Later that afternoon in the shop Charlie sidled up to Tony when no one was about and said, "Tony, I'm right pleased for you. It's always nice to have someone to write to." He paused. "But you'll let me have a look at them photos, won't you? I mean it was me that put you onto her."

"Charlie, I can't. Are you any different from the others?"

"Well, no. But I won't let them know, Tony. Don't be silly."

"No, Chas, I can't let you look at them and not the others."

"Tony, I'm your mate. I gave you her address in the first place, remember? If it wasn't for me..."

Tony always left him with a glimmer of hope and he had Charlie hooked up for two days trying to work him round.

Karate was different. No one liked him enough to want to play any practical jokes on him, but we had to devise a scheme to shut him up. Apart from his rants about Straffen, all manner of other things could set off another diatribe. He was always reading books about Hitler and praising all things German. Black men, Jews, communist countries, screws...he wanted to exterminate everyone except himself and the German race. At the drop of a hat he would be foaming at the mouth and it got all of us down. In particular Roy.

Roy came up with the perfect gag by using something that we knew about him. Before I had been transferred to Durham, the cons had barricaded themselves in their cells. After a few days, the screws had jacked off some of the doors, then the rest had come out under their own steam. But, however you came out, everyone got a belting before being slung in another cell. Karate had been one of them but, when they got to him, he was in such a funk that he crapped his trousers. One of the screws had shouted out, "We've got someone here who's shit himself!"

Karate thought none of the other cons knew, but a few of them had heard the shout and, later, the screws were only too glad to confirm its owner. Naturally no one rubbed his nose in it; however obnoxious a man, even cons baulk at destroying him for no reason. So Karate came to think of it as part of his buried past. Until Roy pretended that he'd seen a memo on Greene's desk that used the incident as a morale-booster for the staff.

The next time Karate started to spoil everyone's lunch, Roy interrupted him and said, "Wait a minute Karate." He turned to Tony but was talking to all of us, "I don't know if anyone knows about this but I was in

Greene's office today, seeing him about my visits, and I saw a memo to the wing staff on his desk. It was about how they should handle us and not to be frightened if we started to get stroppy. One bit read, 'They are not so brave. In the demonstration of July '68, one of the inmates excreted in his trousers as he was being led out of his cell.' Tony, you were in that demo. It wasn't you was it? You didn't *pony* (shat) your *strides* (trousers) did you?"

Tony played it perfectly, "No. I was one of the first whose door was jacked off. I didn't hear it but I got told about it later. You were there Karate, did you find out who it was?" The only other person out of us seven who'd been in the barricade demo was Karate, but he studiously ignored Tony.

I cringed for Karate, who had gone very quiet and was absorbed in eating his lunch. Inevitably Roy doubled up on him.

"I notice you ducked Tony, Karate. It wasn't you who crapped in his strides, was it?"

Karate looked up and replied quietly, "No. No. It wasn't me. I didn't know nothing about it."

"I wonder who it was, then?" Roy said, grinning all over his face. "Imagine – *ponying* his *strides*. What a show-up. 'They weren't so brave.' He rolled the phrase around like a mouthful of vintage malt whisky. 'They weren't so brave.'"

Charlie picked it up. Whether physical or psychological he couldn't pass by the chance to torture someone. "Ahum, it sounds a bit strong. Roy, do you think they made it up? What do you think Karate, do you think they made it up?"

"Don't know," Karate said, even quieter. I had to hide my face behind a newspaper that I picked up; it was wicked. But it was funny and it worked. Whenever he got the rants again, someone would bring up the catchphrase "They are not so brave" and go into the developing folklore about the incident. How the stench lingered for days in the wing and how the screw who discovered it had to go on sick leave.

Roy used to revel in it. Having been a mate of Fraser, he had a strong scatological sense of humour and always found the incident a source of great delight.

That was how we used to fool around. I was a victim too but one of the privileges of writing up the history is that you can censor your own embarrassment.

****

Summer drifted past in an untroubled haze: we played tennis, badminton, lifted weights, cooked the occasional meal... Time passed.

About the middle of the summer, the screws' tea-boy, a six-monther from the main prison named Brian came up to Roy and me to ask about something Charlie had said. He was an OK guy and as he was in the wing all day with us we had become passingly friendly. We were having a cup of tea in the Twos' TV room and he came in to have his ten-minute break with us.

"John, Charlie told me that if I went to the newspapers when I get out, I could get some money for a story about this place?"

Roy and I looked at each other warily and Brian flushed up – he knew something was wrong.

Roy asked, "How much did Charlie say you could get?"

"He said I could get four or five grand." His eyes had a pool-winning glint and he emphasised the sum incredulously.

I was puzzled as this didn't fit Charlie – he hated publicity. "What did he say, then?" I asked.

"Look, don't say anything to him, will you? I promised him I wouldn't tell anyone else. But you know what Charlie's like, I don't know if he's having me on or not. That's why I asked you."

Roy told him, "You won't get four or five grand, Brian. Perhaps four or five hundred quid."

It was still a lot of money to him and as he was going out soon to nothing the odds were whatever we said he would try to flog his story. Charlie had planted a fecund seed in rich soil. But we still didn't know why. So we took Brian through everything Charlie had said when he had planted the idea.

Brian said, "He told me to tell them that he was the nicest fellow I'd ever met and that his last words to me were, 'Don't come back; it's a mug's game.'"

Roy and I nearly had convulsions. Brian looked mystified as he didn't understand Charlie's game. I said to Roy, "Do you realise we've stumbled on a genuine Charlie classic? Charlie watchers everywhere will celebrate our name forever more for giving them this one."

"John, I think you're right and this will definitely go down in *The Charlie Book of Diabolicals* as a classic." We talked like this sometimes, egging each other on.

We told Brian the way the Sunday tabloids operate. "They'll pump you about the wing and, then, write it up the way they want to. You'll sign a contract to the effect that their version is the only one that will get you any dough. They want sensationalism and you won't be having any control over what's published."

He assured us that he wouldn't let that happen and that he wouldn't let them write anything bad about us.

"Yeah, try and leave Roy and me out," I said knowing it would make no difference.

About a fortnight later Brian was discharged. The next Sunday Roy came into my cell with the *News of the World* and there was a barrow-load of garbage in it about everyone in the wing. I read it and we both went to see Charlie who was in his cell on his bed with Lawrence in attendance.

"Have you seen your handiwork, Charlie?" He grabbed it but, in his eagerness to find the bit that he'd primed Brian to feed the press, he forgot to fake some outrage. After he'd seen the plugs for Charlie weren't there, we got the outrage. "What do you mean my handiwork?" he said belligerently.

"Charlie," Roy said pedantically, "when you put the idea in his head the cleaner came and told us about it."

"Well, he's a liar. I didn't tell him to do that. Do you think I'm fucking mad? No one hates publicity more than I do. It was Stafford who told him to do it." Trust Charlie to go unerringly to the best available alibi. Dennis Stafford had been in the wing for a time while the cleaner was there, but had been transferred well before this incident.

"Charlie," I said wearily, "he even told us about the bit you told him to put in about yourself – 'the nicest fellow he'd ever met.' Remember?"

"That was Stafford. I was there when he mentioned it once."

I rubbed it in. "Charlie what about the other bit he was supposed to say you told him: 'Don't come back;

it's a mug's game.'" Roy joined in chorus with me as I said the words.

"It was Stafford. You know he loves publicity. I wouldn't do a thing like that, on my kids' eyesight." Doubtless Charlie's formidable progeny, the result of a complicated train of couplings, are grateful that their eyesight is not affected by their father's oaths.

He was starting to lose his temper. His eyes were darting around, he had sat up on the bed and he was muttering about "fucking people telling lies" about him.

"All right, Chas, we'll pretend it ain't even in the paper," I said. Then, Roy and I walked out.

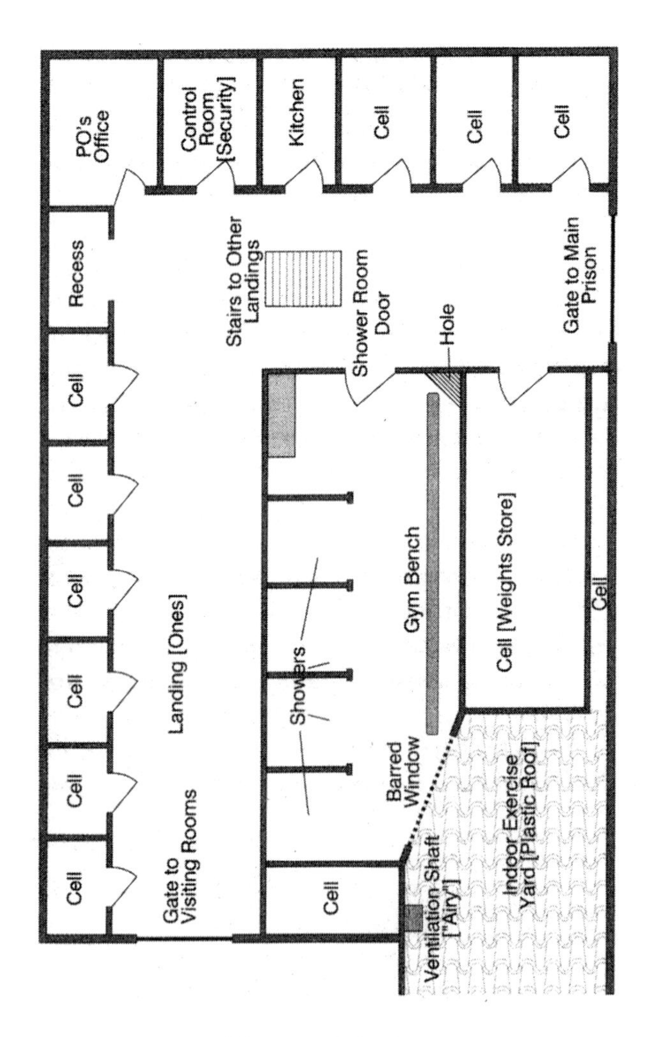

Diagram of the Ones

Chapter 6
Charlie joins the dig

Roy had been nicked with Charlie and before that he had worked for him since he was fourteen years old. At their trial Roy had been offered a trade by which he wouldn't get any time if he went *QE* (gave evidence for the Crown). Roy turned it down. I'm not saying he deserved something for refusing to grass, but Roy drew ten years and even Charlie had been moved to promise him his scrap yard business when he got out.

Roy wasn't that close to Charlie at this period. For the first time in his adult life he'd become independent of him, but nagging at the back of his mind was Charlie's commitment. Meanwhile, Charlie gravitated to Lawrence whom he dominated completely. Lawrence followed Charlie round like a lapdog. After Charlie thought up a scam to get out of the wrought iron shop, they even began making soft toys together in the wing. They were only apart at night.

I was with Roy a lot of the time, but I argued and discussed things with Tony and I was friendly with Wally. There was no bad blood between any of us, but Charlie was coolest towards me. It always fell to me to jolly Charlie along to pull his weight with rota tasks like washing up or to check him from taking more than his share of the rations. I didn't like policing him but he disliked me more for doing it. There was a tension between us, although it would have needed a sharp observer to notice it. Wally couldn't stand Charlie because they were natural opposites. Wally would never climb on someone else's back to achieve something, whereas Charlie did it instinctively. They avoided each other.

I'd already made an arrangement with Wally to *make one* (join the coup) on an escape if anything came up. Wally always talked escape; his mind continually proofed prison security for loopholes. He'd thrown up a few ideas, but none of them had come to anything. Out of the whole wing, the area we'd identified as the most promising was the shower room. This was the only place in the wing where you were left alone or unobserved for any length of time.

E-Wing was a milch cow for the staff. There were three or four screws to every con. Every landing had at least two on duty, usually lounging around by the bridge catwalk at the right angle of the L-shape of the wing. On the Ones there was always a bunch by the PO's office or the control room.

The shower room was situated on the Ones, roughly on the inside corner of the L, with one window facing out onto the inside exercise yard. It was a big window, three feet wide by six feet high, about five feet off the ground and reaching nearly to the ceiling. It was heavily barred and meshed with tubing that was electronically wired to set off an alarm in the control room if the circuit was broken. The outer wall on the inside of the L, instead of forming a sharp corner, made a short diagonal section and this was what the window was built into.

The shower room had a conventional half-windowed, household door that opened inward off the bottom landing, the Ones. It was more or less opposite the stairs that went up to other landings. On either side of the door were big windows about three feet square, so that the shower room was wide open to inspection. However, the only ventilation was the window onto the yard or the shower door if it was opened. When anyone took a shower, the door was always closed – it could not be locked – and generally the window overlooking the inside yard was shut as well. As the ventiliation was poor, the hot water would quickly steam up the door window and the two windows either side of it and, if any screw looked in from the Ones, all he could see were fleshy blobs. Thus, potentially we could work in the shower room.

There were four shower stalls on the right-hand side as you came in and opposite them was a long wooden gymnasium bench that we used to change on. There were also a couple of standard issue cell tables in the room. The floor was concrete and it would have needed a pneumatic drill to go through it. This just left the walls around the outer window that overlooked the inside exercise yard. But these were built of stone blocks about three foot thick and as impregnable as the floor. Wally and I endlessly proofed the shower room but gave up in the end.

At the beginning of September, when Wally and I were showering, he said to me, "John, have a look at that, and tell me if you think there's anything unusual about it." Wally liked this oblique approach to things but his tone indicated he'd found something with escape potential. He pointed to the corner nearest to the door on the left-hand side as you came in. The window to the left of the door stopped short about three feet of the side wall, but instead of the wall continuing on to meet the side wall and forming a rectangular corner, it ran across in a diagonal, thus cutting out the corner. I had never noticed anything unusual in this and, even looking at, I didn't until Wally explained it to me.

"That corner has been cut off for a purpose. They never do anything in the nick without a reason, John, however stupid the reason may be. It's either a ventilation shaft, or an old chimney that's been bricked up."

He had already checked that the same structural oddity continued through the Twos and Threes and, he thought, probably through the Fours as well. With the monsters up there, it was off limits to us and he hadn't been able to see for himself. He suggested that we should make an examination of the diagonal wall: put a probe in to see if there was a space behind it. Although it was intriguing, I didn't see the mileage in exploring this structural anomaly.

"But, Wally, we're in the middle of the wing. It doesn't take us anywhere."

"I know, but all the same it must lead somewhere that would. It might go into the cellars below us and we might find a weakness there that could take us out of the wing. Or it might be possible to crawl right up it and come out on the roof. We don't know until we find out."

I reluctantly agreed, though to me it seemed futile. The next day, after the others had showered, we took a small metal peg from the weight-lifting stands. Wally chipped away the plaster until an edge of a brick was uncovered. We quickly fell into a pattern of work by which Wally operated on the hole, while I kept lookout. The low gym bench was about a foot high and ten feet long. The practice was to push it as far as possible against the wall opposite the shower stalls to avoid the shower splash. However, the diagonal section we were working on and the lay of the window overlooking the inside exercise yard meant that the bench would not sit flush against the wall. It would start at about the middle of the diagonal wall we were working on and run down the shower room to the granite blocks surrounding the exercise yard window. The gap between the bench and the side wall was about 18 inches.

When we went to work, I'd pull the bench out slightly and sit on the end of it by the shower room door. This gave me a panoramic view of the Ones, Twos, the stairs and also the screws congregated around the control room. Wally would crouch behind me and the bench; if I saw someone coming towards the shower room, I would warn him and he would scramble up and get into a shower stall well before they opened the door.

During his brief stay, Dennis Stafford had pioneered the steam bath. With the bad ventilation, running the showers at their hottest turned the shower room into a Turkish bath and some of us would lounge about in there for an hour at a time. The screws had become accustomed to this even before we started to probe the diagonal wall. But to allay suspicion, Wally and I made a habit of opening the door every twenty minutes or so, and asking the time or shouting out for something. The result was that the screws hardly ever bothered us in the showers. If they wanted to do a check or tell one of us something, they would open the door and from the doorway look in to make a body count or deliver the message. Naturally, they didn't want to come inside a steam room in their uniforms.

Thankfully, the shower room door opened inward and was hung on the side we were working. Moreover, the angle of the diagonal wall that we were working on was too acute to be seen by someone standing in the open doorway.

Everything was on our side: the steam, the bench, the way the door opened, the reluctance of the screws to enter, but most of all the location of where we were digging. The screws on their daytime rounds would only check the outside window and wall and never looked at the wall on which we were working as it so obviously did not go anywhere with escape potential. In fact, once we'd started, I realised that our little cut-off corner was the only possible place in the wing where we could work undetected.

It took about two days to dig through the partition wall, as it was two bricks deep. But Wally made a hole big enough to poke a piece of wire in to probe whether there was a shaft behind the bricks. There was and it seemed to be quite small – about a foot across. As the shaft had to be triangular in shape and we were coming in at its widest point, it was more likely to prove a dead end than a way out.

When it comes to escaping, Wally leaves me in the kindergarten. A couple of months previously he'd obtained permission to keep a hamster, a funny little thing that always seemed to be asleep in the daytime. However, Wally hadn't got it as a pet, but because of the scope it gave him to smuggle tools in and out of the wrought iron workshop. He made a metal cage for the hamster in the workshop and built into it a false bottom in which he could hide digging tools up to nine inches long. He would make spikes and hide them in the workshop, then he would take the hamster's cage into the workshop to fix its treadmill, which naturally the hamster was always wearing out, hide the spikes in the false bottom, which easily beat the search and the metal detection screening when he left.

One time, when the cage went in and out about three times in a week, the screw who was doing the searching said, "What you feeding that hamster on, Wally? Spinach?" By now, all thoughts of anyone making anything productive in the workshop had been abandoned, and all anyone did was make things for fun.

The other device that Wally introduced that was crucial to our escape plan was his papier-mâché hobby. He would sculpt heads out of the stuff and also made an adventure playground for the hamster on a couple of three by two-foot food trays that he appropriated from the prison kitchen. There were tunnels and hills and a little maze. Papier-mâché is made from pulped up newspapers that are soaked in water for a couple of days. The obvious place to store the bucket containing the papier-mâché was, of course, the damp shower room. In fact, Wally's bucket of papier-mâché had become a fixture in the shower room even before we'd started our dig.

Anyhow, we soon had a routine of showering that avoided the others; we'd usually spend about three-quarters of an hour a day working on it. We plugged the hole with papier-mâché but it was taking too long to scrape out the mortar between the bricks and we had to start chiselling. We asked Tony Dunford to help us. I'd hump weights up and down outside the shower room – where in fact I'd always had my work-outs – while Tony would stand-in as Wally's watchdog as he hammered away with a five-pound weight at a chisel-like spike. The screws had long been used to watching me weight-lifting on my own in an almost ceaseless series of mindless exercises, so this again fell in with our plan.

As Wally prised out the cement around the first brick, the light grey of the dried papier-mâché began to stand out against the blue paint of the wall, so the next problem was to get some paint. I cleaned out a jam-jar, then I asked Roy for some light blue emulsion. When he got bored in the afternoons, he liked to re-paint a cell. Naturally he asked me what I wanted it for.

"I'm going to paint the mirror in my cell," I said.

He shot back at me, "Don't take me for a mug, John. Charlie takes more pride in his cell than you." Charlie's cell was a cesspit.

I was hurt that he obviously felt betrayed by me. I had neglected him as I was spending more time with Wally and in turn he was drifting more towards Charlie. I tried to waffle about genuinely wanting to do a bit of painting.

"OK, you don't want to tell me but you're at it with Wally. You're always in conference together, then you're both in the shower a lot. And you're not up each other (having a homosexual affair). So what's it about?"

"I can't tell you yet, Roy." He shrugged and gave me the paint.

At this stage neither Wally nor I wanted Charlie in the coup, although we knew we might need him later on. It wasn't merely that neither of us liked or trusted him but he'd already blotted his copybook by refusing point blank to fund another of Wally's schemes. He'd condemned it out of hand because he was worried about being cheated out of the money we'd asked him to put up. Nevertheless, we were living in cloud-cuckoo land to believe he would not eventually work out what we were up to. Roy, for one, might tell him.

Pretty soon we got our first brick out. Then came a couple more on either side, which revealed another layer of bricks behind the wall we were working on. It took ages to strip out the bricks from the second wall and we had to up our work rate. We would work over lunch-time, which was 11.30 am to 2.30 pm, then at the weekends we'd have a long session in the afternoon and another in the evening. After about three weeks we got a blackened brick out and felt a faint breeze of cool air. Suddenly we were in business. I would get palpitations at night thinking about it.

The shaft was a bricked up chimney, which was all sooted up. However, the shaft got narrower as it went up, so it meant we had to go down. A lighted match showed that was where the breeze was coming from. We had to make the outside hole bigger to dig at the floor of the old chimney. We had only taken out three bricks from the third row up from the floor. Now we had another three from the second row and two from the fourth row. The hole was already getting quite big.

The logistics of removing the bricks, then after a session replacing them and disguising the hole's appearance became extremely time consuming. Aside from the eight bricks on the outside of our diagonal, all the other bricks from the inner wall had to be taken out to get at the chimney floor. When we finished a session, they all had to be replaced, then the eight outer ones carefully re-stacked, wedged with prison socks, and covered with papier-mâché to the level of the surrounding plaster, before being painted with blue emulsion. The final result, though, was impressive as the hole looked like a patch of wall infected by the fungus that plaster sometimes develops in a damp atmosphere.

After about a week, we had stripped the inner wall of bricks as far downwards and sideways as you could reach. Now you could thrust your arm and shoulder in and reach the soot and rubble lying in the shaft, but even probing with a chisel we could not reach the bottom of the chimney. We started to scoop the soot out, and washed it down the outflow of the washroom, but we needed somewhere to dispose of the stones and bits of brick in the shaft that were preventing us from getting at the source of the current of air. The bricks from the inner wall were also piling up and needed to be dumped. Nevertheless, the breeze meant there was some kind of hole in the bottom of the chimney that we could probably open up.

At the end of September, we got our first alarm call that this was not going to be a straight forward dig. Charlie and Lawrence put their soft toy number on hold and went into the workshop to make some wrought iron gates for one of Charlie's women. A few days later Charlie sidled up to Wally and said, "Look, I have been looking at the shower room and I think we could dig our way out of there onto the yard. Will you *make one* with me and Law?"

Wally replied, "Come off it, Charlie. Where can you dig out in the shower?"

"Through the wall by the window."

Wally replied incredulously, "Through three foot of granite! That's crazy. What will you use to dig through that?"

"We're making a proper tool now."

"It won't work. You can leave me out of it, Chas."

When Wally told me all this I dismissed it as silly Charlie talk. But Charlie isn't silly and I was too wrapped up digging through the wall to read the writing on it.

The next day Wally saw Lawrence making their tool – it was done so he would see it. Wally, though, was more interested in how they would get it through the metal detector. Unlike him, they had no safe means of masking metal. They chanced their luck. Charlie put it inside his vacuum flask: if you put a flask on the floor a negligent or forgetful screw could pass the detector over you, then watch you pick up the flask and forget to screen that too.

And it was another Charlie classic. As they were waiting to be searched Charlie, who had some papers and a jacket in his hands, handed his flask to Tony and said, "'Take this out for me, Tony."

Tony took it without thinking, but Wally had been keeping Charlie under *obbo* (observation) all morning and had seen the tool go into the thermos flask.

He muttered to Tony, "Don't take it. Give it back to him." Tony took one look at Wally's face and went to give the flask back to Charlie.

There was no way Charlie was going to have that flask – he ignored Tony, scuttled up to the screw to get searched and said to Lawrence out of the side of his mouth, "Law, take my flask from Tony, will you?"

Tony plonked it into the arms of the now panic-stricken Lawrence who was trapped with no out. He was surrounded by three or four screws, and there was no one left to pass the flask on to. He was lucky though – the screw never passed the metal detector over it.

When Wally told Tony what Charlie had done, he was incandescent. He grabbed Charlie by the shoulder in the TV room. "You just set me up to do what you're too gutless to do yourself. There was a tool in that flask." The terrible thing for Tony was that the prison authorities would have assumed that he wanted the spike to stab another con. It would have put years on when he might be considered for release on licence.

Charlie was unperturbed, "Don't be ridiculous. Do you think I'd do a thing like that to you? There's nothing in the poxy flask. Who told you there was?" He ordered Lawrence to get the flask, which Charlie flashed under Tony's nose. "Look, there's nothing in it."

Even after Wally had told me all this we still couldn't work out Charlie's game. That evening, Charlie again asked Wally if he'd like to *make one* to dig out of the shower room. Wally again said no.

We were worried, but comforted ourselves with the knowledge that Charlie wouldn't have the guts to dig out. The next morning Charlie and Lawrence played badminton. Afterwards, while they were showering, they prised a lump out of the wall at the bottom of the last shower stall. Wally saw what they had done after lunch. He came straight up to my cell to tell me. He was almost crying with rage and frustration. "The dirty slag is trying to get us nicked," he said. We both inspected what Charlie had done. He could not even dig out where he had prised the piece of plaster off the wall. But that didn't matter, this was Charlie's blackmail card.

I was just as angry as Wally. We walked up to Charlie's cell to confront him in the middle of his web. He was lying on his bed, facing the door; Lawrence was sitting on a chair next to the bed. We walked in and I asked calmly, "Charlie, you digging a hole in the shower?"

He just looked at me for a moment, weighing up

the propriety of the question, then answered, "Yeah."

Wally couldn't contain himself. "You can't dig out where you've started, Charlie. You're not even on an outside wall," he said accusingly. But logic has never caught Charlie out.

"Yeah, that's right," replied Charlie. "We're going to branch left when we get a little way in. Why are you so excited about it? I can dig out if I want to, can't I?'

I couldn't restrain myself any longer. "Charlie, you know we're working in there. Don't take me for a cunt."

Charlie was getting there. He had got us to admit that we were already digging out. "I don't know anything about you working," he said.

I started to move into threat mode. Any moment the finger would start wagging. "Look, just leave it out. After we've had our pop, you can have yours. We started first."

"Why haven't you put us in? We'd have put you in. I've already asked Wally if he wanted to *make one*, and he said no."

He was sitting up now, gesticulating in self-justification. "What's the matter with you people? I'm in here as well as you, ain't I?"

"That's bollocks," I replied. My temper was beginning to take over. "You just leave it out."

"I'm not leaving it out, son. You dig your hole and I'll dig mine. Won't we, Law?'

Lawrence never even looked at him. He just sat there, staring at Charlie's cell wall.

The finger finally started wagging as I said, "Alright, Charlie. Let's stop playing games. If you don't leave it out, I'll break your jaw."

He jumped off his bed and stood before me, "You'd

better do it now then."

"I'm warning you, Charlie."

"Well, don't warn me. Do it."

We were like two warring kids in the playground playing "hit me first", only we both had a purpose. I was trying to frighten him and he was trying to blackmail me.

"Come down to the TV room," I said quickly. Sometimes if you can get people on their own they will cave in, but in front of others they will fight to avoid losing face. I walked out of the cell with him right behind me. There was a screw on the landing. We were both too agitated to be able to hide it and he watched us both with interest as we went into the TV room.

Straffen was looking at *Watch with Mother*. He took one look at my face and stood up warily.

"John, go outside for a bit and shut the door," I told him. He did as he was told. Then I said to Charlie, "Chas, you're grassing me. I know exactly what you're doing. You're blackmailing Wally and me to put you in our scheme." Like Wally with his logic, I was using prison values to shame him to do the right thing. But the right thing for Charlie is always what Charlie wants to do.

"I'm not grassing you. How am I doing that? I just want to get out of this rathole, just like you. Do you think I want to spend twenty stretch listening to these Geordie cunts?"

"But you're grassing me, Charlie. You're digging a hole that's bound to get tumbled, and they'll rip the place apart and you know it." There was a touch of despair modulating my anger.

"Look, John, what are we arguing for? It's fucking silly. We can blot Lawrence out, just put me in it. I'd do the same for you if it was the other way round."

He was pleading with me now in order to give my pride a way out. *Watch with Mother* was blasting away. Charlie's betrayal of Lawrence refuelled my anger.

"I won't let you do it to me, Charlie. I've told you. I'll put it on you."

I cocked my fist, he was glaring at me. We were only about 18 inches apart. I could see fear in his eyes but resolution to stand his ground, too. I pushed him with my left forearm. He retreated a step, then pushed back at me defiantly with his chest.

"Well, go on then, do it," he said, taunting me.

He was wound up like he had been on the night of the barricade. Some people can give me a free punch but Charlie doesn't figure amongst them. He was sure I wouldn't hit him, sure enough to offer his chin. But not certain. I could see the tension as he waited to find out whether he had read me right. I pushed him again, shifting my weight as if I were going to throw one. It made him suffer a bit more, but I knew I wasn't going to hit him. His breathing was laboured. Charlie is one of those people who become rigid and inflexible in the face of threat – he still made no move to protect himself. But he stayed with his bluff until it won the hand.

"You know I'm not going to hit you," I said. I turned and walked out of the room. As I walked onto the landing I saw the same screw who saw us go in. He was leaning over the railing opposite, staring greedily at the door. I went down to the Twos and into my cell, feeling cheated and defeated. A moment later Wally came in and asked me what had happened. I told him.

"There was nothing I could do, Wally. He's got us by the balls. We've no choice except to put him in."

"Lawrence as well?" Wally could hardly bear it. Charlie's bonehead lapdog.

"Yeah. But neither of them are going to get out. We'll fuck him at his own game."

Wally nodded in agreement. "Yeah, we'll think of something. He is a dirty slag. I can't believe anyone could be so devious. And treacherous." He shook his head in wonderment.

That afternoon, in the shop, Wally told them we'd agreed.

In the wing, I told Roy what Charlie had done. I felt depressed even though we were just a few bricks away from the chance of freedom. No one had ever done anything like this to me. What I was feeling was what I had seen in men whose mates had turned supergrass and put them in prison for twenty years.

Roy told me he hadn't told Charlie about the plot. He had tumbled what was going on before I asked for the paint. "John, he sniffed it out for himself. It is obvious. How the screws haven't tumbled it is a miracle."

I believed him. Not because I wanted to either. I just knew him and we had been good mates. You make an unspoken pact with some men. You back each other up whatever the cost. It's a male thing, I guess. But it's there and always will be. He didn't tell Charlie.

I asked him why Charlie had done it.

"He's desperate, John. He's got that South African bird and everybody's pumping her up except him. You know what he's like with a bird. I know him; it's killing him. He was never this bad outside."

Roy and I were close for a while but he had to side with Charlie – that is where his future lay. But I always liked Roy. The only time I wobbled on him was one time when we were watching some crappy True Brit film on TV about a WW2 spy who had been tortured. She – it was a woman – had held out under electric shock torture by the Gestapo. Roy said, "That's bollocks. It's impossible."

I was hardly following the plot but as I am by nature contrary I reflexively said, "She could have... it's not impossible. Women are supposed to be able to withstand pain better than men. So some of the scientists say."

"What are you on about? John, I know."

"What d'you mean, you know?"

He replied, "I was with Charlie, don't forget."

I had forgotten. "Oh yeah." Then I queried, "But what do you mean?"

"When you put people under the electrodes, they go. They tell you everything."

I knew that Charlie had acquired a hand-cranked generator that was used for sending out SOS signals when he cut up for scrap a WW2 bomber. This was the machine that was used on his victims.

Roy seemed to be in a confessional mood and he didn't need much prodding from me to elaborate. I asked the obvious question that even when people supposedly confess how do you know they are not lying.

"You know. They can't lie, which is why this (the film) is a load of bollocks."

I asked how you can tell.

"Yeah, people lie because you want stuff from them that they don't want to tell you. But you know that. So you push it to when they have to tell the truth, when they can't do anything else."

I expressed my puzzlement.

"They can't take it anymore, John. They turn into little kids and ask for their Mummy. It's something that you have to see to know. But they can't lie to you. Even months later if you go into a pub 'cos you have to see them they go back into it. They're broken and it never mends."

I felt the cold, clammy clutch of something horrible…I didn't look at Roy, but kept watching the stupid black and white movie. His confession dried up and we never spoke about it again.

The ironic thing was that Wally and I had been on the verge of asking Charlie to come in with us. We had already asked Tony to do more than we should have. He did not want to escape. At twenty-two he was resigned to spending maybe the next thirty years in prison. We were going to have to get rid of the bricks and mortar soon. This would mean taking stuff up to our cells and chucking it in bits and pieces out onto the pathway outside the wing, so events were forcing a recruitment drive.

I told Roy that we would have had to invite Charlie to join us anyway. Then I added, "I can't let him do this to me, Roy. He won't get away with it."

He just looked at me without comment. I was blustering to salve my defeat.

That night I was sitting next to Charlie in the armchairs in the TV room. We were watching the news while we were waiting for the cook to come in. He started to ask me about the hole and how long it would take before we escaped. It was like we were pals and that afternoon hadn't happened. I answered him gloomily, shrugging my shoulders and grunting the occasional "maybe" or "I don't know".

"Still, John," he said, "when we get out I'll see you alright for dough and you can come to South Africa if you like."

This was too much for me. I looked at him and smiled, "Charlie, we both know how you got on this firm. You blackmailed yourself in, so don't let's play make-believe and pretend we're pals."

He didn't say anything; nor did I. And that's where it rested.

The next day, when Charlie wasn't about, I buttonholed Lawrence. I tried to make him feel ashamed of himself for being a party to this threat to expose us if we didn't put them in the coup. He blamed Charlie. "You know what he's like. I said it was wrong, but he never takes notice of what you say."

I led him on to tell me how Charlie had behaved when he first tumbled that Wally and I were up to something. Charlie had worked it out himself – Roy never told him. He had heard the chiselling, which sometimes didn't synchronise with the weights. Lawrence told me how Charlie kept going into the shower room trying to find our hole, but couldn't find it. He mimicked the terrible state Charlie'd been in searching for the hole but never looking in the right place.

Of course, he'd never looked at where we were digging as it was at the wrong end of the shower room. But as the time went past, he got more and more in a panic never knowing when we might take off. That was when he hatched his "my hole" plot to flush us out.

And it worked.

Chapter 7
Payback for Charlie

All four of us started work on the hole. The first task was to clean out the bottom of it. We scooped out all the loose bits of brick and pebbles, then put them all into one of the two-gallon urns that prisons use for transporting anything liquid from the kitchens to the wings. We carried it up to the TV room and stood it in a corner to the right of the door. No screws came into the TV room and we had the lights off, so there really wasn't any risk. Our only concern was Karate – the only one of us who didn't know what was going on.

Wally collected a pile of newspapers and started wrapping up small handfuls of stones in twists of newspaper. The plan was to take about six packets, go to one of the three lavatories on different landings and push the packets one at a time past the bend in the pipe and flush them away. Karate could see that something was going on, but not what. Wally had a table in front of him with the can between his legs making up the parcels.

Wally gave us all strict instructions: one flush of the lavatory for every little packet of stones. Tony did a trip, and then I did, and then we waited for a while for Charlie to do one. Nothing might seem more conspicuous than relays of men going to the lavatory and all of them flushing it half a dozen times, but screws are not looking for patterns in the bowel movements of cons. When Charlie collected his parcels, he went to the lavatory next to the TV room. Even with the TV on, we could hear it flushing. After two flushes, a screw walked past the door and stood in front of the recess.

"Been flooded out then, Richardson?" We could hear everything.

Wally erupted as quietly as he could, "The cunt, the fucking cunt. He always does what he wants to do."

I shot out. There was water all over the recess with bits of stone and grit awash in it. The screw was staring straight at it. I grabbed some floor cloths from one of the buckets that Roy and I used for our cleaning, then started to spread them over the worst part. Tony, Roy and Lawrence came out and, with Charlie looking extremely sheepish, it wasn't long before we cleared it up. When we got back into the TV room, Wally pitched into Charlie but keeping his voice low so Karate would not hear. "I told you and told you to flush them one at a time, and you go straight out and do the opposite." Wally had told us what would happen if we didn't.

For once, Charlie copped a plea. It must have been a first. "I'm sorry, Wally. I thought it would be alright. Flushing the khazi in there, I thought the screws were bound to think there was something wrong." I never said anything but I remembered Roy's words when we were told that Charlie was coming back to the wing – "You don't know what he's like." I fucking knew now.

Wally was like a dog with a bone. "You've got to listen to me, Charlie. You'll get us all nicked. There's going to be a lot more little things like this. You've got to be more careful. You've got to listen to other people. One tiny mistake and we lose everything."

By nine o'clock we had all the stuff flushed away and the can cleaned out. We took all the large pieces to our cells to throw out of the windows. They were installing some kind of heating system, the pipes of which were being laid underground outside our cells. There were piles of dirt and rubble and we gratefully added our humble offerings to them. The next day was Saturday and we decided to get rid of some of the bricks, which were developing into a logistical nightmare. All the loose bricks we'd prised from the inner wall of the partition had to be pulled out every time we worked on the hole, then packed back in when we'd finished.

After closing the hole this day, we left eight bricks out for disposal. Lawrence went to get a tea urn and the only one he could find was the one which Straffen used in the kitchen to fill the electric boiler that was always on for making tea. Filling it up was one of the jobs that Straffen had commandeered and he kept the empty tea urn handy to get water from the tap. I put the bricks in it and replaced the lid, then asked Charlie to return it to the kitchen, which was more or less opposite the shower room. I wanted to leave it where it normally was as once we had finished papier-mâchéing the hole we would open the shower room wide to clear the steam, thereby speeding up the drying of our false plasterwork. Keeping the can in the shower room with the door open could catch the eye of some helpful screw who would think what's that doing there and grab it or something.

It was a marginal risk but you play it tight when you have to, which was why I wanted to take it upstairs myself. The screws were used to seeing Roy and me carrying tea urns. I was just putting my clothes on and purely by chance I looked over to the kitchen and saw Straffen in there, holding the lid of the can and staring at the bricks. I nearly had a miscarriage and I wasn't pregnant. I tore over to the kitchen in my bare feet.

"John," he said to me, pointing at his urn, "someone's put bricks in it and I can't fill the boiler." Straffen made a ritual of everything and everything had to go like clockwork; if anything interfered with the hands he'd get wound up.

I took the lid from him and replaced it. "Don't worry," I said. "I'll fill it up."

"But I fill it up at three o'clock every day and now I haven't got a can. Someone's put bricks in it."

He was angry because someone had hijacked his poxy can. I was shitting a brick myself at the thought of some screw coming in and hearing him.

"Get upstairs," I said roughly. "I'll fill the tea-urn today but in the future I'll make sure there's always a tea-can down here. I promise you. So go upstairs.'

He didn't like it. He went off muttering to himself and I went back to the shower room.

I called Wally down. I told him about Straffen, the tea urn and the bricks. I said, "He is going on about his fucking tea can and the bricks in it. You'll have to talk to him." He was laughing. "What the fuck you laughing at? It's not funny."

"Your face is. Don't worry about Straffen. He won't say anything to a screw. He hates screws." Straffen has numerous white scars criss-crossing his bald head where the screws used to cosh him into submission after they'd goaded him into a panic.

I finished dressing, took my gear upstairs with the

paint-pot and put everything in my cell. Then I came down and filled the tea-urn with a big saucepan. After that I took the can full of bricks up to the Threes' TV room, which was the only room with a wide enough gap between the bars to get a brick through. Eight bricks weigh rather more than an urn of tea. I only had a vest on and I was conscious of the veins popping out of my arms and forehead.

I tucked the can into the corner of the room and either Wally or I stayed beside it. When it was dark, Wally kept watch for me while I threw the bricks onto the rubble outside. As I did so I thought what a fucking pantomime this is – if Johnny Public only knew what we escapees have to go through to give them a vicarious thrill, they'd grant Wally and me a free pardon.

The next day we flushed a lot of water down the hole by filling plastic bags from the shower, then emptying them down it. This cleared whatever passage the breeze was coming from, as it blew a lot stronger. I'd taken my hand at digging now and again, but Wally did nine-tenths of the work. He really slaved at it. Charlie and Lawrence helped only with the little things that had to be done every time we went to work: keeping watch, using the weights – usually my job – handling the bricks, giving Wally the tools he needed.

Wally widened the entrance hole, so that he could get his head and shoulders right inside and dig with two hands. To see better he'd made some fairy-lights out of bootlaces and mailbag twine wax. He'd rest one on a jutting brick and really get to work. He'd located the entrance through which the breeze was coming and you could push a digger down it and meet no obstruction. We couldn't tell whether this meant it was a narrow duct or an opening into a larger space. But this really made us feel excited and I began getting butterflies. After my Chelmsford debacle, I couldn't believe the gods could be so kind.

The opening was to the left, and three feet down at an angle of forty-five degrees. In order to work on it, Wally had to remove more of the bricks on the inside of the shaft, so that it widened out all the way up. A couple of times I went inside the shaft myself, more to see how we were getting on than in order to work. Inside, I felt positively claustrophobic, as you were more or less wedged in and could only come out in a slow twisting crawl. But working in the deepened shaft meant that Wally could not get out quickly. Now when someone approached the door, I could warn him but he could not extricate himself from the hole in time to make a show if they opened the door. This meant that whenever anything looked iffy all he could do was freeze.

This worried me and I wouldn't let Wally stay down there for long. I didn't like Charlie and Lawrence keeping watch for him either because they were too careless. Yet, for all my care, it was when I was on watch that our worst scare came. It was lunch-time and the same PO I'd grabbed at the barricade came striding over to the door of the shower room. "Freeze, Wally," I said. PO Nichols opened the door. I was sitting on the bench, smothering the hole. Wally's legs were stretched out on the floor, hidden by the bench, behind which all the bricks were also stacked.

Nichols looked to me and asked, "Is Wally in there, Mac?" It was a fucking count.

I looked uninterested and said, "No." My answer

wasn't good enough for him. Instead of calling out to the landings, as most screws would have, he walked into the steamy shower room and looked into all the cubicles. I felt everything falling apart. I was sure that when he turned to come back he couldn't possibly miss the hole. I got up and followed him and as he turned I locked him into eye contact.

"I told you he's not here," I said, "what on earth made you think I'd lie?" I held his eye as he walked away and he missed the hole, which to me had a big flashing red arrow pointing to it. As he left, I said to Wally, "Get out, I'm going to try to draw him into the office." I grabbed a towel and followed the PO out.

"Is it okay if I weigh myself?" I asked him. The scales were in the PO's office and a screw always accompanied you when you used them. I knew exactly what the score was. Once Wally extricated himself, he would have to duck out of the shower room and sneak into the kitchen or the weights room before surfacing.

I walked into the PO's office, but he didn't buy it. Instead of tracking me he bellowed up to the landings, "Twos! Threes!" This was answered with a chorus of "Yes sirs!"

"Is Probyn up there?" he shouted. I was panicking. I rushed back to the shower room eyeballing danger to Lawrence and Charlie who were using the weights on the Ones. Wally was now in one of the cubicles.

"Can't you sneak out?" I asked him. "Nichols has looked in here already. Duck into the weights room?"

"I've tried already. If Nichols isn't looking, the other screws on the Ones are," he answered.

"I'll try to draw them into the office again," I said. I walked out. The PO was getting his answers down from the Twos and Threes very quickly. It was a small wing and there were so few inmates that it only took thirty seconds.

No Probyn!

The PO was beginning to panic as well. "Where can he be?" he said, virtually to himself; but he was worried. Probyn was the escape risk. The other screws on the Ones had come alive and were looking up and down the wing. Wally could not get out of the shower room without being spotted. I knew that at any moment there would be a general alarm and an organised search for Probyn, which would mean they would hustle us away to our cells with all the consequences that would have for discovering the hole.

I walked into the office, again trying to distract the PO's attention, but again he took no notice of me. I actually got on the scales before thinking that I had already done this once. I was like a headless chicken not so much waiting to be plucked just roasted. Then Nichols went back towards the shower room. I followed him. The game was up. The steam had all more or less dissipated now and the hole was impossible not to see. It wasn't just a flashing arrow, it was a talking hole – *Look at this hole these naughty cons have dug.*

Nichols walked along the cubicles and in the third one was Wally. He still had on the overalls he wore to protect his body from the rough edges of the bricks. The shower was running! As if that wasn't bad enough, there were streaks of soot and dirt running all over his face and body. I was standing beside the PO. Wally had the sick look of a fugitive who had been flushed out.

The PO's relief was palpable. He said reproachfully, "Wally, you've been hiding again. You really gave me a fright this time."

Wally picked it up like greased lightning, "I fooled you, didn't I?" But his change of expression to a teasing mischievous look was so hammy that to spare everyone the embarrassment I just wanted to hold my hands up and say "fair cop". But Nichols was so relieved to have found Wally that he was blind to the evidence before his eyes. He just turned and walked out without looking at anything, shaking his head and smiling to himself.

I shut the door as he shouted up to the other screws, "It's alright, he was hiding in the showers." There was some context for the PO's take. Sometimes Wally used to play tricks when a count was taken – it flattered his vanity to get people worried that he'd escaped.

I looked at Wally. As my head stitched itself back on to my torso, I said flatly, "You've still got your overalls on." His look showed he didn't know.

"Fucking hell, John," he said shaking his head at what we'd fluked.

Charlie and Lawrence came in now. Charlie said to me, "Corblimey, didn't you see me trying to warn you? There's all black down your back and neck." I'd had a dabble at the hole, so I was streaked like Wally! We put the tools and the spare bricks back in the hole, then plugged and papier-mâchéd before painting it. The hole was now gnawing away at my nervous system. I kept going into the shower room to kind of pray to it, to will it to let us out. I ate, breathed and slept the poxy hole: it was my psychosis that only escape could cure.

The next day I made Wally leave it alone but stay hidden for long periods to see if the staff were suspicious. But no one took a blind bit of notice – the incident had just been one of those things. The day after that we got stuck in again. Wally was getting to the opening through which the air was coming. On October 10th, he widened the shaft into the air hole and discovered it wasn't a small passage but an opening into the corner of the cellar beneath the showers.

He soon opened it up sufficiently for us to throw our rubble and spare bricks down into the cellar. While this was great for the logistics, the problem was that the hole's entrance in the shower room was getting bigger.

Wally really smashed into it now. For about a week I tore my guts out snatching and jerking the big Olympic barbell up and down on the Ones, making as much noise as possible. I had the weights slightly loose, so that they would chink and rattle, but to my ears they sounded nothing like as loud as the dull thuds that came from the hole and went echoing round the wing. Lawrence and Charlie were minding Wally and they used to give me the horrors with their slipshod attitude. Whenever I stopped humping iron, there was always a slight delay before they told Wally to stop hammering. They didn't have a clue about this sort of thing.

By the middle of October, Wally told me the opening would soon be big enough for one of us to drop down into the cellar. I eased Charlie and Lawrence out onto the weightlifting while I minded Wally; we didn't want Charlie to know how well things were going. We still intended to fuck him.

However, as the tension built up, Wally and I started bickering. I wanted him to drop down but he said it would be too difficult to get back up. I tried to do it but got stuck – I was bigger than Wally – and it took all of a quarter of an hour for me to get out. The pressure was getting to us. We didn't know where the cellar led to, which meant it could still all turn into a wild goose chase.

Then, on October 20th, Wally widened the opening enough to make it possible to drop down and get back up again. The next afternoon, we went into the shower, opened the hole and he dropped straight down. He was gone for ages, maybe twenty minutes. I was watching and waiting assailed by mounting waves of panic. Any check would be disastrous, irretrievable. I could hardly bear the excitement as he came back up.

"Well?" I said. He was grinning all over his face, but proceeded to fill up the hole and didn't answer. "Come on, tell me," I said.

He shook his head. "No, I'm going to make you wait." We worked on filling the hole with me persistently trying to draw him out. I was so consumed by the hole that I couldn't read his manner. Obviously, it was good news.

The cellar led to an external ventilation shaft – called an "airy" – that came up in our indoors exercise yard where we played badminton. The system was now defunct but originally it worked by drawing air in down the shaft and into the cellar where it percolated up through the landings. We knew this airy well as sometimes when we were playing badminton the shuttlecock would land on the grid and drop down to the bottom. We would retrieve it with a weighted hook. It was about a yard square, so we would have no problem climbing up it. At the bottom of the shaft was a grilled window that led into the cellar that was underneath the shower room. Thus all we needed to do to get into the exercise yard was to cut the bars on the cellar and jemmy the padlock.

I said to Wally, "We'll need a hacksaw then to cut the bar in the tunnel. The paddy will be easy – we'll lever it open with the diggers. But where can we get a hacksaw?"

He paused for a moment, preening slightly, "I've already got one."

"What? You can't have," I replied. The one thing it was impossible to nick out of the workshop were hacksaws. They were guarded like the crown jewels.

"Yes, I have. I've had it ever since the island. I brought it hidden in the box I carry my gear in."

I wanted to kiss him but, first, I am not in the habit of kissing men and, second, you never know with Wally – he might have kissed me back. Suddenly everything fell into place. There was another windfall from the cellar – there was an old broken step ladder down there, which would be handy for coming up the airy shaft. We could get out of the wing and into the main prison grounds, where all that was required was to be able to scale the wall.

That was all. After Chelmsford, I got the heebie-jeebies thinking about throwing hooks up onto walls.

That day we hammered out exactly how we would perform. The first item on the agenda was Charlie. He had been getting suspicious at the way I had eased him out of coming into the shower room while we were working. I'd noticed that in the evenings he tended to follow me or Wally about. Charlie was too old a hand at fucking people not to suspect others of doing it to him.

We decided to tell them about everything except the hacksaw and to make Charlie and Lawrence responsible for getting one in. We had a conference with them. They were as excited as we were, and no doubt relieved to have their suspicions allayed. They never dreamed we had a hacksaw already and they immediately started planning all sorts of schemes by which Lawrence would get one in on a visit.

Wally and I knew we were committing ourselves to breaking out before they either got a hacksaw in or, more likely, Lawrence got nicked trying to do so. We both kept up the pressure on Charlie to get Lawrence on the case. Operation *aitch* (hacksaw) threw Charlie completely off the scent. He was the source of something that was vital for us to make it, so his manner towards Wally and me changed completely. We were now trusted members of his gang.

Sidelining Charlie was now easy but Wally and I still had lots to do. First of all we needed a good rope with an attachment for getting over the wall. This was to be stored down the hole. We put that together on the Friday before we went. Wally stayed out of the workshop to do some sewing on the machine we had in the wing. He made up a good rope from a new pair of sheets – I tested all the joins. Then before the others came in from the shop and while Roy was upstairs, we went into the showers and made up an attachment on the pendulum principle for slinging over the top of the wall and holding there while we climbed up.

We used a strong piece of broomstick with a five-pound weight at the bottom and the sheet-rope tied on the top. We tested it on one of the brick partitions that divided the showers and I also got the feel of it to satisfy myself that I would be able to throw it over the wall. The fiasco at Chelmsford still haunted me.

We dropped the rope down the hole, then papier-mâchéd it back up. Then, just before the others came in the workshop, I got the library unlocked. The plastic fibre-glass roofing that covered the inside yard fitted tightly all round against the two sides of the wing, the wrought-iron shop and the blank wall. It was vaulted and the inverted V at its apex ran across the library window. The library itself was only a cell fitted up with wooden shelves and was at the end of the Twos next to the office where we'd staged the barricade demo.

When we came up into the inside exercise yard we were going to have to climb out of it by a rope dropped out of the library window. This was the only window in the wing where you could get at an edge of the plastic and make an opening to climb through. Once again the gods favoured us: it was a fluke that this happened to be a cell I had access to. If it had been an empty cell, there would have been problems.

I went into the library and got up at the window and started making a gap wide enough to climb through. The plastic was extremely strong stuff, but brittle, and when it broke it ripped and crackled like a machine gun. But we were on the countdown now and what had to be done just had to be done. I made a reasonable gap and went out and shut the door.

On Sunday we decided to saw the bar of the tunnel to the airy and jemmy the padlock of the gate with one of our diggers. We did it after dinner, when the football was on. It was weird being more worried about Charlie than the screws. Wally went straight down as before and, soon, I heard the rasp of blade on metal. It sounded harsh and rough, but to me it was a choir of angels. We'd arranged a code of banging on the floor to bring Wally up, but any count or check would have brought down the curtain on us. Then there was a silence. The sound had only lasted for perhaps two minutes. I wondered if the blade had broken but I hoped that Wally had already got through. I went over to the yard window and listened through the wire mesh that was supposed to ventilate the shower. Then I heard the rattle of the padlock, a beautiful sound that made my pulse thunder. I knew we were going to make it now. This was it.

Wally came back – he had only been gone seven minutes. Laconic and professional, he just said, "I've done them both, no trouble." We bricked up, plastered and painted. Wally had sawed the bar, bent it back, climbed through with the step-ladder, propped it up against the wall, stepped up on it and prised the padlock off. It broke easily, but luckily still held together when pushed shut. Then he took the step-ladder back and bent the bar back.

We went upstairs and made the last few arrangements. He told me that because of my bulk I might have trouble negotiating the hole, so we decided to widen it the next day at dinner-time and go that night. A rope had to be made for dropping out of the window and I said I would do that, then there was our personal clothing to be prepared. That evening Tony and I were sitting in Wally's cell and Wally asked him again if he wanted to come with us.

"It's going to work, Tony. We can't miss. This is your last chance."

"No thanks," he said. "I've got nowhere to go and I wouldn't know what to do when I got there." He grinned ruefully. I felt sorry for him. He was 22, he had spent the last six years in prison and maybe he had another twenty, even more, to go. Yet he didn't even want to escape. It was a hard way to do your time.

But Wally had a look on his face that meant an argument. "John," he said, "I know what you're going to say, but I think we ought to put Charlie in. If we don't, it means that we're going to have to go out blind." He meant our not being able to have Roy and Tony watching for the day patrols before we actually went up the rope in the badminton yard and onto the plastic roof. I started to interrupt but he stilled me.

"No, listen to me. We can do what we like when we're over the wall. We can put the bar over his head in the cellar if you like and leave him down there," he laughed wolfishly. "But we need everybody's co-operation to make this work as well as it can. I'm more worried about him than I am about the screws."

"Wally, think how you'd feel, if he made it and we got nicked? Don't forget his money will count much more if he is out there."

"I know all that," he said. "But I still think we should take him. It's too dodgy not to. If we go down there and he sniffs us out, he'll start yelling and screaming so as to grass us. You know what he's like." The number of people I'd heard say about Charlie: You know what he's like. Tony was listening. He smiled cynically when Wally made the remark.

"I don't want his help," Wally continued, "but I'm not going to let him spoil everything. All we've got to do is to spring it on him now, the day before. He'll have to come."

"What about the other mug? You're forgetting about him." Charlie was bad enough but the thought of bringing Lawrence along too was too awful to even consider.

"Yeah, I know. He only wants to get his name in the papers, not to get away," Wally replied. He shook his head. "Maybe we can blot him out."

I was determined not to take Charlie. Just mixing with him was like tolerating someone who had given evidence against me. As the spectre of him coming with us loomed, I did what I always do when I compulsively have to get my own way – I upped the ante. "Wally, I'd rather not go if you've got to take him. I'd rather go up and smash him all around his own cell. Then we'd both be out of it and you could go on your own. Anyway, that's how strong I feel about it."

Wally knew my brinkmanship routine. He did not buy my bluff of making Charlie a personal vendetta that came before getting out.

We fell silent. Tony now intervened, "Wally, I know it's none of my business, but I think John's right. It would be wrong to let Charlie go." He nodded his head judiciously and said, "He's pulled too many strokes."

Wally's expression showed the uncertainty that was plaguing him, gradually he came round to our view. "Alright then, we'll blot the slag out. But I'd have loved to take him in a way. It would have got up their noses so much. Can you imagine the screams? It would have been worse than Blake (the Soviet spy who escaped from Wormwood Scrubs in 1966). Think of it. *Torture Gang Boss Escapes!* It would kill them."

Wally was a bit of an anarchist and I saw his point. Nevertheless Charlie's fate was now decided. All that remained was to put down the hole the few special garments we wanted to change into when we went. We couldn't start walking around with pullovers and black T-shirts under our arms in case Charlie saw them. We'd decided we'd do it that Monday afternoon, after we'd widened the hole. I was nearly twenty pounds heavier than Wally and he was positive that I'd need more room.

Both Wally and I were completely confident in our ability to make our way out of Durham by foot. We could both hotwire a car, we both had experience of the kind of travelling we would have to do before we stole a car or jumped a train or whatever. We were both opportunists, fit, resourceful, used to deprivation and capable of just hunkering down in a ditch or a shed for as long as it takes. Durham was not a problem now – Charlie still was. We knew he'd grass us if he tumbled what we were about.

Monday lunch-time, we got Charlie and Lawrence working out with the weights while Wally and I widened the hole. Wally told them both that he wanted them both to go down to the cellar during that week so as to make certain they'd have no trouble the evening we went. Lawrence was supposed to cop for a hacksaw on a visit in a few days time. They didn't have a sniff that anything was awry. Just before lunch I'd stashed a bucket containing our Jeans tailored from cotton overalls, pullovers and black long-sleeved T-shirts in the shower room.

We opened the hole up and Wally went to work inside it for about quarter of an hour, then we widened the front opening till it was a good two feet high and three feet across. Then we dropped the clothing into the cellar wrapped in sheets and closed the hole up. It was getting to the limit of what papier-mâché would cover; it was sagging quite a bit in the middle and really looked an eyesore.

When Charlie saw it, he was immediately suspicious. He knew that Wally wouldn't have enlarged it like that without a good reason.

He said to us, "How come you have made it that big? That's asking for it." The screws checked the shower room everyday and without any steam this great big stretch of wall that had been papier-mâchéd over should have been discovered. The big thing in our favour was still that this corner of the shower room was such an idiotic place to dig. No one in his senses would ever have dug there, and the screws never troubled to check it.

But I left placating Charlie to Wally. Wally said to him, "Charlie, I want that Lawrence to go down there tomorrow or Wednesday and I'm not having him getting stuck down there. You know how clumsy he is. It's bad enough having him with us at all, without his fouling it all up into the bargain." Charlie laughed and seemed satisfied with Wally's explanation even though it did not make sense. Lawrence was still a long way from bringing in the hacksaw.

On the afternoon of that same Monday, a con named Joey Martin was transferred to the wing. He was a London robber who was doing life. Although I didn't know him, I knew people he knew. He was *sound* (reliable) and a tough nut, but also a hothead who had killed two people. His current life was for shooting a guard during a robbery in 1965.

In my book, any gunman who can't control an unarmed man without killing him shouldn't be allowed to carry a gun. Quite apart from the barbarism of taking life unnecessarily, the Joey Martins of crime are a menace to work with – they turn armed robbery into murder. As a consequence the hunt is far more comprehensive and, if anyone is convicted, they draw life.

On the outside I steer clear of trigger-happy robbers, but as a prisoner Joe was fine. He'd been in E-Wing before, and had taken part in the barricading of the cells on the occasion when Karate had that unfortunate accident in his trousers. A screw told me that when they took them out of the cells Martin was the only one who put up a fight.

He was still on punishment for an attempted escape at Leicester's special wing. This meant that he should have been confined to his cell, but I managed to get him unlocked and he came into my cell to have a chat. He began telling me how unlucky they had been at Leicester. I was interested to hear all about it as Eddie Richardson had been in the coup. Then out of the blue, he said, "Is there anything going on here, John?"

Normally I would not have given anything away but what with everything that had happened that day, the Charlie headache and the suddenness of his question, I reeled a bit. I said, "Not really." But I had obviously given the impression that there was.

However, Joe immediately backed off and apologised for even asking. "I'm sorry; I shouldn't have asked. I was out of order." This was a correct observance of the proprieties. Joe was doing it right. The right way to serve your time is to keep your nose out of other people's business.

I said, "No, Joe, it's nothing. You surprised me, that's all. You're entitled to ask. I'd do the same."

So we dropped the subject. Afterwards, I told Wally that I'd shopped myself a bit. Not that Joe had a clue what actually was going on. But I explained what had impressed me, "But as soon as he got my reaction he backed off and accepted that he couldn't be put in. Compare him with Charlie."

"Yeah," he replied. "Joe's a nice fellow. I knew him down the Moor. I was going to suggest putting him in, but it's up to you."

"No, it's not up to me, Wally. He's game enough; I honestly don't mind." Joe had already shown himself as sound, as one of your own, someone you could trust, someone who'd back you up, someone who wouldn't grass you if he was nicked and you weren't.

There is a deal in every walk of life. In that respect, criminals are no different than any other group. But I had never mixed with scum like Charlie and Lawrence who'd only honour deals that they had to or that suited their interest. I knew their kind – treachery is an ever-present feature of organised crime – but I would rather be in prison or graft on a building site than be like them. I nodded my agreement to take him as it was right.

This meant postponing the break for a day, which proved politic as Charlie had started to track our movements again. That evening I got Joe out of his cell, then filled him in on what was going down tomorrow evening.

He couldn't comprehend what I was saying. He kept saying "Tomorrow?" over and over again.

"Yeah." I broke through his bemusement, "Do you want to make one?'"

"You must be joking. Do I want to make one? Of course I do."

I told him about Charlie and why he was banned. He accepted it all, but he was worried about how he was going to get out of his cell for long enough without giving us away. I told him that wasn't a problem as we'd arrange for him to have a shower. I said that if it didn't work out, then we wouldn't be able to take him. He also accepted that without question.

The next day a weight-lifting referee came to the wing and I did a couple of lifts for an inter-prison competition. I weighed exactly 175 pounds and I broke my personal best for the dead lift. I was definitely fired up. The rope I'd made the previous day for dropping from the library was hidden in the laundry basket. I retrieved it and took it up to my cell. The cook was due over on Tuesday evening and, about a quarter of an hour before he came, I told Joe to get himself unlocked and go to the library. He rang his bell; the screw unlocked his door and let him in the library before wandering off to his station on the bridge across the landing. I went to my cell, wrapped the rope round my waist, then wandered over to the library. While Joe kept *obbo* for the screw coming back, I moved a table up to the window, jumped up and tied the rope to the bottom of a vertical bar and dropped the rest through the hole I had ripped in the Perspex into the covered exercise yard.

It was dark, but if someone inspected the yard they would see it. This, however, was unlikely and now we had to push our luck. I briefed Joe on a few details of the plan but he never knew whether he was coming or going and I didn't have time to tell him very much. I left him there, then went down to the weights room to look across the yard where I could just see the rope dangling down. I reported to Wally that everything was in order.

Then the cook arrived and we all went down except Joe and cooked a mixed grill: chop, bacon, sausage, chips, tomatoes. My stomach was jumping like I'd already eaten a jack-in-the-box. The thought of food was almost nauseating. I tried to act normally but couldn't. Usually, at such times, I'd be stalking Charlie to stop him staking out the best chop, filtching the bacon or getting at the milk. This time I stationed myself at the sink and just peeled the potatoes. I was feeling tense and irritable.

It had to be tonight and as always the waiting was the worst part of it. Will my nerve hold out? One day when I need it, the gameness just won't be there. Whenever I'm waiting for the off, I dread that this might be the time. I have seen people crack on the plot. It's a sight that no one – least of all the culprit – ever forgets. There are memories that can make a life not worth living.

We finished cooking about half past seven, shared out the food, and retired to the TV room; Wally took the food we'd pulled out for Joe along to his cell. Again he told him to have his shower in about quarter of an hour's time; Joe had already had the nod from the PO on this. Charlie and Lawrence settled down in their armchairs to eat their food while watching TV. I tried to eat something but my mouth was not producing any saliva and the food turned into indigestible lumps. Even though I might not be eating for a few days, it was no good force feeding myself. I sipped some milk instead.

It was mine and Roy's turn to wash up. I started collecting the trays and I said to Roy that I would do it tonight.

"Don't be silly," he said, "I'll help you." He began to pitch in.

"Leave 'em, Roy," I said. "I'll do it." I was ratty. He wandered off. Meanwhile, instead of settling down to watch the TV, Charlie and Lawrence went upstairs to the Threes to work on their soft toys. They worked in a double-cell room directly above the showers. Although it was two landings above the plastic roof, their workshop overlooked it. If they looked out they would not be able to see us come up as the angle was too acute but they might well hear us. The Charlie problem was on the front burner again.

Wally told me this as I was finishing the washing up. We were committed now, so we had to live with Charlie almost certainly hearing us on the plastic roof. Wally left me, then went along to Joe to tell him to come down to the shower room. I watched them enter. The idea was for me to join them a couple of minutes later. As I was waiting, Roy came in. He'd sniffed out that something was going down.

"Have you finished?" he asked.

"Yeah."

"Coming up to watch the box?"

"No. I don't fancy it tonight." I was champing at the bit but he was still hanging around. Roy picked up on coups. He'd seen too many not to get a feel for something like this. Finally, he went back upstairs. I came out of the kitchen and over to the shower room. The windows were already steamed up and Wally was unpacking the bricks from the hole and passing them to Joe who was stacking them behind the bench. Parked in the middle of the shower room, though, was an exercise bicycle that Roy had used that afternoon to make the weight for the competition. It bothered me; it was out of place. But it was any minute now and I didn't want to trundle it out onto the landing and put it into the weights room.

Even before I'd taken my shirt off to ease my way through the gap into the cellar, Roy came striding in, leaving the door open behind him. He went over to the bike. Wally has a high-pitched, rapid-delivery cockney that goes into a whine when he is agitated. As he was now. "Roy, what are you doing? Watch that door. Are you trying to get us nicked?"

Roy stood by the bike looking puzzled at Wally and Joe who'd both stopped dismantling the hole. Wally had his martyr's face on, while Joe looked apprehensive. Roy was mesmerised by the implications of what he had stumbled on. We were all fully dressed, not unclothed as we normally would be for working on the hole. And there was Joe.

I was standing next to Roy who turned away from the others and whispered to me, "Why did you tell Martin?"

The noise of the showers drowned his words from everyone except me. "It was Wally's idea," I replied. "He wanted to put something away that we'd left out and we had to tell Joe."

Roy wrinkled his brow in bewilderment but still didn't move.

"Roy, come on," said Wally. He held his arms out beseechingly. "Take the bike out. You'll get us nicked."

Roy picked up the bike and carried it out of the door, which I shut behind him.

Wally said, "John, he'll tell Charlie."

"It's too late now," I said, tugging off my shirt. I was going down in my underwear and shoes, so I would not snag up on the bricks. I wriggled into the cleared hole, then eased myself into the opened-up corner of the cellar. But my shoulders stuck and as my feet were still outside the shower room hole I could not get any purchase to lever myself through.

"Wally, I'm stuck. Push my feet in" Wally bent them up and got them into the hole; I braced my feet against the back of the chimney and forced myself through the opening into the cellar. I slithered through and caught hold of a steel girder running along the cellar roof, which Wally had already warned me about, and swung down on to the floor. In the dark I fumbled for my bundle of clothes that we had dropped down the day before. While I dressed, Wally dropped down followed quickly by Joe. I gave Wally his bundle and said, "Get the rope."

"I've got it already," Wally answered.

Wally went ahead and I pushed Martin behind him, "Hold on to him, Joe." The three of us crocodiled through the debris on the floor of the cellars, which were connected by archways in the walls. Then we reached the tunnel that led to the bottom of the ventilation shaft. We had to crouch as we moved along it. Wally reached the bars and bent back the one he'd cut and pulled the step-ladder through. Joe was next, followed by me. Wally was already going up the step-ladder. He opened the padlock, swung back the grill and stepped out onto the yard. Joe followed, then I joined him. We were still putting clothing on.

I pointed out the dangling rope leading to the plastic roof to Joe and said, "Joe, up the rope and don't make any noise on the plastic roof. It crackles like a machine gun."

Joe started to climb up, while Wally prepared to follow him. But when Joe went through the hole I'd opened up in the plastic roof, he made a terrible racket. Wally winced beside me. He started to go up carrying the other rope dangling round his waist. I followed. Neither Wally nor I made any noise on the plastic sheeting. As I came out Joe was balancing on the office roof, backing towards the section of wall we wanted to make for. I started to crawl towards him, but he waved me back with his hand and then started to come back himself. When he was near me, he said,

"There's a screw with a dog looking towards us. He must have heard us on the plastic. We'll have to go the other way."

This was across the plastic roof and past our wing and the remand section which abutted onto it. This would take us towards the front gate but we had not been able to recce this part of the prison and we did not know if we could climb over the wall there. The way we'd planned to go we knew was okay, but now we had to take our chances in uncharted waters.

Joe picked up one end of the rope and Wally the other, then they went across the plastic roof. It crackled like a Gatling. Guys in the remand wing started appearing in their windows silhouetted by their cell lights. Then I heard Charlie shouting from the wing, "Bastards. You bastards…"

Wally said, "Hear that cunt?"

"I hear him. We knew he'd grass us if he got the chance," I muttered. I don't know if Wally heard me but I could hear Charlie hollering and hooting. He was going to make sure those screws knew.

We reached the end of the roof and dropped down. We could see the wall but this section had a continuous reel of barbed wire attached to the top by brackets. The ground had just a few patches of grass and through my trainers I could feel it cold and damp. We were moving just by what we could see. We didn't know where we were going.

We came to the end of the remand wing, and then to our left we could see the wall, which ran into a high building that at its highest was thirty-five feet. It was the court house that was built next to the gate. The nearest part was only one-storey.

We ran towards it. Wally put his foot onto the

window-sill and got up on the flat roof. That led to a higher part of the building and looked easy to climb. I got up and turned to take the rope from Joe, but before he could move a screw came round the far corner of the wing and grabbed him from behind. "Alright, alright. I've got you, don't move." Joe didn't struggle.

"I'm sorry, John," he said. He looked exhausted and nodded his head in resignation. "Can you give me the rope?" I asked. He fumbled at his side, but the screw smothered him and other screws were arriving by now. "See you, Joe," I said, then ran towards Wally.

He was in the far corner of the roof, looking up at the next obstacle. The roof ended at the wall, which was only about ten feet from our vantage point. The trouble was, it still had barbed wire on the top. To our left, though, the next section of the court house rose about ten feet but about six feet from the top a line of foot-long spikes jutted out horizontally. I pushed Wally up and he grabbed the spikes and heaved himself over. I took my pullover off and threw it over the spikes and tried to pull myself up, but the pullover kept tearing.

"Wally, double it up." He was leaning over but every time he heard a whistle go or a walkie-talkie crackle – and there were plenty of both by now – his head would turn aside. I thought for a moment he was going to leave me. He twisted the pullover and leaned over, holding it out to me. I grabbed it, scrambled up, got hold of a spike in one hand and let go of the pullover, but I couldn't seem to lever myself over the spikes the way he had. Wally had moved away.

"Wally," I called.

He looked round at me. "Come on, John."

"It's the fucking spikes," I laughed. He came back and hauled me up by my shoulder over the spikes.

We were on a flat concrete roof, which had guttering on the side. Ahead of us were more rising vaulted roofs. There were whistles and sirens going now. We went towards where we knew the outside was, traversing various roofs and gulleys. Then we came to a section that overlooked the outside. There was a small wall that was a continuation of the main wall but was obviously only decorative. We both looked over the rounded top of the wall. We could see a patch of open common opposite but below us were about twenty screws. Anyway this section was too high to drop off without breaking an ankle or something. We were nearly 30 feet up.

We pulled back smartish but still one of them spotted us. "There's one of them," we heard him shout.

"What do you think, Wally?"

"Don't know." There was a cornered look in his eyes. Everything was coming apart. I wondered if he blamed me for not taking Charlie and perhaps ruining it for him. The screws were marshalling to cut us off.

"I'm going this way," I said to Wally and I took off towards the still rising roofs. I was thinking that once I get over them, then they must at some stage slope down and, anyway, this direction would take me away from the screws we had just seen. After going about ten yards I looked back and Wally wasn't there. He'd gone his own way. I went on for about fifty yards and the rooftops were descending. I knew then that I wasn't in the grounds of the prison as all the usual devices to stop climbers were absent. Suddenly I was looking down into the gardens of a row of terraced houses. Behind the wall at the back of the gardens was a small cobbled road.

I had to get down a sloping tiled roof that ended about 10 feet off the ground.

I could see freedom and I knew once I made that road I would make it to London. I scrambled over the roof making some noise, then I dropped down into the gardens. The nick was behind me and to the right – I went left towards the cobbled road. Then I heard the clatter of boots on the cobbles and I peered over the fence – there were about 15 screws running along the road coming from my right and going left but they cut left again obviously towards the continuation of the prison wall. When I could no longer hear them I took their route but as I hit the junction where they turned left I went right. Away from the prison.

I was running at middle-distance pace. But I could feel all the reserves in the tank. I was 28, a superfit powerhouse running from a 23-year jail sentence.

Only a bullet could stop me now.

Chapter 8
Escaping

I ran over a hump-backed bridge towards a well-lit street. On my left was a blank wall but to my right was a police station! It had an illuminated blue and white lettered sign jutting out from the side of the wall: POLICE. It didn't concern me – it was eight o'clock, dark and I was in a built up area, I could lose anyone. But there was no activity anyway. I wondered if the prison authorities knew I was on the street yet.

When I reached the bridge I looked back: it was all completely dead. Ahead of me were the lights of a semi-major road that swept round to my right and a single-decker bus was slowing down to cross the road I was on. If I'd had any money I would have caught it. Instead, I crossed the road and ran left along the pavement of the main road towards another road that branched off right in roughly the direction from which I'd come. But on the pavement, about fifteen yards before the turning, a young man in a blazer had stopped and was looking at me as though he knew something was up.

I thought for a moment that he was going to try to grab me. I ran towards him. I was hyped up and confident of just ploughing through him if he did try anything. However, I checked myself. My euphoria at being free was making me reckless.

I slowed down to a respectable jog, which made it look like I was merely hurrying rather than running from trouble. He stepped aside as I reached him and I turned up another road generally going away from the prison. I was now on a narrow climbing road, shop-fronted on both sides. I was still moving too quickly as people were looking at me. It could not be the way I was dressed as I had on dark nondescript clothing and trainers. Maybe it was more the expression on my face that was attracting attention. But I wanted to get out of the town centre and into the cosy hiding options of the suburbs and countryside.

After a hundred and fifty yards, the shops fell away and I came to a small unlit common to my right. I plunged into its enveloping darkness and slowed down to a walk. I was on a diagonal dirt path; ahead of me was a church and a sprawling graveyard; on my right a line of trees. I looked back at the road and saw a car, which had come from the same direction as me, pull up beside the common. It was packed with dark blue uniforms.

The balloon had gone up and the hunt was on. I ran towards the sanctuary of the trees.

This time I did run. Not flat out, just off it. I knew I must not shoot my bolt by taking off in a panic. There was a long way to go. What fear I had of the pursuing police or warders was dispersed by the sheer physical power of my running. I had cause for my confidence at being able to outkick any pursuers. I wasn't up to club athlete standards but, at 2 minutes 10 seconds for 800 metres, not far off it.

I reached the trees and felt the sanctuary of their protective branches. Suddenly I was treading on air and I went down in a tumbling fall. I had overrun a steep drop in the ground! As I hit the bottom I cursed myself for my carelessness. I slithered to a halt among some bushes and saplings but I knew I'd injured my left wrist. There was no pain, but I knew I had. I wondered if anything else had gone, which the adrenaline was obscuring. I was on the bank of a river.

Then I realised I had lost a shoe! I swept the ground around but no luck. I kicked off the other one. By now I knew my only injury was my wrist and, lucklily, that was just sprained not broken. I was acutely aware, though, how my stupidity had turned the odds against me. I was slightly injured and I had no shoes for the long, hard slog to safety.

I heard the river lapping softly below me and gingerly I made my way down to the water's edge, then eased myself in. I swam across with a gentle breast stroke. It was about twenty yards wide and in the middle I felt exposed and easy to spot but with some underwater swimming I made the other side without raising the alarm. It was October and cold but I didn't notice the chill of the water. I crawled up the bank on the other side and froze, taking stock of my new circumstances. I was now shoeless, injured and soaking wet. I had to be more cunning, no more charging around in the china shop.

It was quiet, but deceptively so as very soon I heard shouts and the voices of a search party with the occasional bark of a dog. I lay doggo. I heard them wading up the river and saw the odd flash of a torch. A duck whirred up in protest. As they were on the other side of the river, I wasn't worried; but I took comfort from the thought that the dogs would be distracted by the flushed out wildlife. I needed a place to hide.

I went up the bank to a riverside path, which I crossed, then I came into what seemed like the communal gardens of a college or university. There were lots of criss-crossing paths, flower beds and lawns. I walked up to the rear of the houses that backed onto the gardens. They were grand Victorian terraced houses that had been converted into student accommodation. I hid under a friendly bush; it began to rain. I heard groups of students returning to their houses. I was there an hour when I heard the sounds of a search party combing the gardens.

I had not been spotted. I knew that…it had to be a routine search that was being mounted because this was the general direction I'd been seen to go in. But it worried me that they were now searching on the correct side of the river. I must have been spotted crossing it. I found a working yard off the gardens and let myself in through the latched gate. The yard was only fifteen feet long by twenty feet wide and was illuminated by the light from a number of upstairs windows. Inside the rooms young men were preparing to go to bed. I found a corner to curl up in and shelter from the rain.

I wasn't worried by the search party. As long as I didn't panic and break cover I knew they would be searching for a needle in a haystack; they would soon move on. After about an hour, an old man came out and emptied some rubbish into a dustbin. He was only a few yards away from me, but I didn't move and he didn't notice me. Then some teenagers came in the yard and entered through the door he'd used.

I decided it was time I found another hidey hole. I went back into the gardens and turned to the left and continued until I found another sheltered place. I lay on the ground, listening to the murmur of young people talking in one of the rooms of a big semi-circular building. I felt like an outcast as I thought about the life they led and had ahead of them against the life I was living. A life of plunder, secrecy, fear, violence, being hunted…

I tried to rally my spirits with the thought that a few hours ago I had been in a top security jail serving 23 years and now I was free with only 300 miles between me and London. It was a kind of miracle, but then it wasn't. I would much rather have been a student like the ones I could hear. I was only about eight years older than them…

It stopped raining. I waited until I felt the emptiness of the graveyard hours. I knew that once I started moving my mind would charge up and my dispirited mood would lift. I went back to the path along the river and walked rapidly along it in the same direction I'd taken before I'd swum the river. The river banks were beautifully landscaped on both sides with grass, trees, bushes and flowers. For about half a mile I was able to go forward freely and easily, but I was conscious that I had to preserve my feet from injury. I came into a factory area where I couldn't keep riverside. Rather than run the risk of taking to the streets, I decided to swim out of the town. Durham isn't a large place and the current of the river was running my way.

I got into the water and the cold hammered my chest like a heart attack, but I told myself I would get used to it. I swam past a half-submerged pipe on which stood a big long-tailed rat, its fur spiked by the water. It watched me with interest, turning its head as I swam past. I smiled in acknowledgement that I was like him...hunted, reviled, but free and surviving.

The cold got so bad that I felt my strength waning. At the most I had swum hardly two hundred yards. I climbed onto a stretch of derelict ground that looked as if it couldn't be reached except from the river. Again I took stock of the mistakes I was making. It was stupid to have got back into the water. At the price of recklessly squandering my energy I had put hardly any distance between myself and the hunt. It occurred to me that watching the swimming events on the TV of the recent Olympic Games had gone to my head. I stripped my clothes off, wrung as much water as I could out of them, then I lay on the ground and waited for my clothes to dry, for morning to come, for seeing some sense.

From where I lay I could see a cinema clock, its hands and numbers illuminated in red. I watched time pass. Morning came... I waited there until seven in the evening before clambering over a crumbling wall that broke under my weight as I dropped down into a cluttered-up builder's yard. I considered breaking into the office and using the telephone to summon up help from London but rejected it. I knew that I must get well away from Durham before I drew people into aiding and abetting my escape.

I climbed over the builder's side gate and jumped down onto a narrow cobbled street, lined with high-fronted tenement-style dwellings. My stocking'd feet did not bother me as the cobbles were smooth and even. I walked briskly, always crossing to the other side when passers-by came towards me. The darkness and my avoidance tactics meant that I did not arouse any suspicion. I came out into a well-lit slip-road that led to a roundabout, which carried motorway signs. I turned away and made for the badly lit back streets. The one I took led me past a provincial bowling alley. It was crowded with youngsters who were pouring out on to the pavement in an eddying, chattering stream, ignorant of how rich they were in freedom.

After about half a mile I came out of the built up area and encountered my first field. I clambered over a fence and started to run. I headed in the direction of a rail track from where I could hear the occasional train. I went north. London was south, so north was the way I was going. Then I came up against the stinking river again – or more probably a tributary – but it was much narrower here and quick flowing. I took my clothes off, made a bundle of them and, holding it out of the water, swam across. In the middle the current tipped me slightly and, as I adjusted my stroke, the bundle shook loose. I watched my socks drop out and float tantalisingly downstream. I almost started ranting at myself for making another stupid mistake.

On the other side, I wiped the water off my body, put my clothes on, and took off towards the railway, avoiding roads and farmhouses. It took me about an hour and a half to reach the track; by then I reckoned it was about half past ten. Once on the railway track I really began to pay for the stupidity of losing my shoes and socks.

The track was laid on a base of flint. Some of the flint-stones were scattered over the sleepers on which I ran. In my eagerness to get some mileage under my belt, I ignored the pain to my naked feet. It drizzled a lot, too. Every time a train came from either direction I scrambled down the embankment and flattened myself into the earth. After about four hours my bruised and cut feet forced me to stop.

I sheltered under a railway arch until dawn, then I walked along the track for about a hundred yards before laying down under a bush at the bottom of the embankment. There was a field next to me.

The morning trains were coming past quick and fast and I kept glimpsing the dining cars with smooth, overweight, dark-suited men, picking at expensive food and drinking coffee. Such different worlds we lived in, but the only part of their world I wanted to join was to be on that train and eating breakfast. About 9 am, a young farmer appeared and exercised his horse in the adjoining field. As with the students I felt a kind of rapport with him but the rain interrupted my musings. Heavy rain quickly penetrates your clothing and suddenly your body heat is not enough to keep the elements at bay. A part of my mind was nagging at me to find shelter but another wanted me to stay where I could not be spotted. I was on the verge of moving a thousand times, but every time put it off.

By the afternoon I was so cold that I had to act. Once I did, I knew that whatever the risk it was the right thing to do. Again I was conscious of the basic mistakes that I was making. I wasn't thinking right. All I needed to do was travel slowly and safely for about three days, then find a phone box and ring for help. Yet while I was moving safely away from the hunt, it was at the expense of wrecking myself physically.

But I had to find shelter. I ran along the railway track for about half a mile until I chanced upon a gangers' hut. Inside, everything had been smashed up by vandals who had inscribed their initials on the walls in tar. The graffiti of impotence.

The hut was a lifesaving refuge in more than just shelter. Inside was an old grey worsted jacket, which fitted me. I stripped off my clothes and wrung them out. I ripped up the granddad-style winter vest that I had on under my black T-shirt and bound my feet. Then I put on my pants, cotton overalls that had been tailored into Jeans, black T-shirt and warm jacket. I lay back on a bench and, while the steam rose from my body, waited for darkness.

About seven o'clock, I took off from the hut, my feet now reasonably protected. I drank some rainwater. Lack of food would not handicap me for at least another three days but I knew I had to keep drinking. Prison acclimatises you to hunger, so I was not especially bothered by not eating. Dehydration was the big danger as it disorientates and handicaps you.

I travelled fast and within half an hour I came to a small town. I was slightly more presentable now; the only eyesore was my cloth-bound feet. But I could pass as a homeless down-'n'-out. I cut off the rail track and walked towards the town. I kept to my criss-crossing tactic to avoid passing anyone close by. No one looked at me strangely. I found a housing estate and I wandered around until I found a telephone box. I reversed charges and rang Jean, an ex-girlfriend of mine, who used to write to me occasionally.

I told her to go round to John Dunlop, a guy I'd worked with on the pavement. I gave her the name of the town I was in, Chester-le-Street, the location of the phone box and its number. I asked her to get a lift organised through Dunlop for 8 o'clock the next morning; I stressed my lack of shoes. Then, I left the telephone to find myself fresh lodgings for the night. I recce'd a small patch of derelict ground that was next to a railway bridge. It had the obligatory big wooden hoarding advertising *Horlicks*. I squeezed through a gap in the fence and sat huddled up on the ground, but again it started raining. Now I had more or less done it, I didn't feel the need to embrace the elements. I moved out of the hoarding site, then walked around until I found a middle-class residential street with garages next door to the houses.

I picked a house with a double garage, the doors of which were slightly open. Inside was a Hillman Minx and two children's bicycles, another back door led into the garden. I looked for a tap inside the garage but couldn't find one. What I did find in the corner was a stack of empty fizzy drink, lager and spirit bottles. I drank the dregs of all the fizzy drink bottles but one had about an inch of flat lemonade in it that to my starved palate tasted ambrosial. It virtually imprinted itself on my taste buds and for a time I was drinking a couple of bottles a day of the stuff. Since then the passion has moderated, but even today the taste of lemonade evokes what I was feeling that night as I waited for the morning and my trip back to London.

I dossed down on the backseat of the Hillman car but even though this to me felt like a bedroom at the Ritz I could not sleep. I timed the moment for leaving the garage accurately. After cleaning up the upholstery I walked out and asked a milkman the time – it was half past seven. I took a slow walk around the area, energised by my rising excitement; then returned to the road where the telephone box was. The kiosk was on a straight road with pretty post-war houses and dainty little gardens on both sides – the best type of council estate. I waited outside the box. Some children emerged from the houses and began going to school, then the last of them was gone. It must have been about nine o'clock. The telephone rang and I went inside the box and answered it.

"John?" It was Jean.

"Yeah, what's happened?" I asked.

"I'm ever so sorry, but the car broke down miles away from anywhere on the way up. I didn't know what to do, so I came back home." I couldn't believe the stupidity of it and began ranting.

"So it broke down? Why didn't you come up by train with clothes and some money?" She started to cry. It transpired she knew someone with an old banger and had recruited him to drive her up.

"I didn't know what to do, John."

"Then for Christ's sake go to Dunlop. You've got to get someone up here today. I can't take another day of this." What I couldn't take was the belief that it was over, then having to adjust to it starting up all over again.

We arranged for her to ring the same telephone box at two o'clock. I plodded back unable, as there were so many people about, to do my criss-crossing routine. The rags on my feet attracted looks of curiosity and distaste from passers-by as they clocked my appearance. I turned into the main road and a woman with a small child demonstrated her repugnance by crowding her child against the fence to make way for me. I wanted to say to her that I was not a leper, but in a way I was.

I had sustained myself for the previous twelve hours on the belief of the lifeboat travelling up from London to rescue me. Emotionally, I could not come to terms with the fact that it hadn't even started and everything had to begin again. I was utterly demoralised, beaten, defeated and I began wallowing in self-pity. I trudged back to my hoarding and wedged myself against it, thinking for the first time that I might be captured.

The time passed with leaden slowness. I could hear a distant church clock faintly chiming the hours. At what I judged to be about half past one, I climbed out from behind the hoarding, taking care that no one saw me. I was frightened by the uncontrollable hopes that began to rise in me again. I waited by the telephone box, but there was no ring. At about half past two, I rang up. No answer. Of course not, they were on their way up by now.

It started to rain, not heavily, just a drizzle. Inside the box it was warm and sheltered. I stayed in there, leaning on the metal stand holding the directory, willing the telephone to ring. People would come up to the box and I'd walk out and sit on the small front-garden wall of an adjacent corner house and then go back into the box when they had finished. I was no longer taking even elementary precautions.

I rang up again about half past three and the operator refused to let me reverse the charges. I didn't even argue with her, because I'd sunk into such a state of maudlin apathy. There was a pain in my chest, my breathing became shallow and rasping and I began to toy with the idea of having myself committed to a hospital. As the afternoon dragged on, this idea became increasingly attractive – a clean, crisp, warm bed, some hot sweet tea, a rich soup…solicitous nurses. It was a reverie that took me over. I kept telling myself that they would whisk me in as an emergency because of my chest condition and I'd be fine as no hospital checks identities.

The schoolchildren had long ago come home and the telephone was now being used quite frequently. Cold and despair aggravated the pain in my chest and I had difficulty in breathing. My behaviour was putting me on offer for someone to ring the police and report me as a tramp who was using the telephone as a dosshouse. But I couldn't cut off from the lifeline that it represented. I was there four hours!

At six o'clock I rang up again and this time Jean answered.

"Thank god you've phoned," she said. "I've been trying to get through all afternoon."

"But I phoned at two o'clock," I said.

"I was late getting back. Why didn't you..."

I interrupted her irrelevant chatter. "What's happening?" There was a guy around twenty-five years old, casually dressed, outside the phone box looking curiously at me.

"They'll be there at eight o'clock. They've got everything you need."

I don't care what mainliners say about a heroin rush, or pools winners say about seven draws or anyone says about sex, this was the ultimate hit.

"Listen carefully," she went on. "They're driving a red Morris Oxford and one of them is wearing a sheepskin coat. They'll stop at the phone box and the man wearing the sheepskin will go inside. They'll do this every quarter of an hour from eight till nine, then they'll go. Be there John, won't you?"

"I'll be there." I put the phone down and walked out of the box. Instead of going into the kiosk after me, the guy who was hanging around walked away. I watched him go but the surge of hope after my despair had desensitised my trouble antennae. Nevertheless, one windfall from the good news was that my breathing had returned to normal and there was some pep in my step. I decided that I'd go with the new pick-up but if sheepskin didn't show I would rely on my own ingenuity. If the 8 o'clock meet proved a no-no, I resolved to steal a car and drive to London myself...and, if I ran out of petrol on the way, steal another one.

As I approached the turning into the road where the hoarding was, two plain-clothes detectives crossed the road coming in my direction. I got them and, as I did, I twigged that the guy outside the telephone kiosk had been a policeman, too. I watched them contemptuously as I walked on. I knew I had nothing to worry about. I'd decided. All the psychosomatic symptoms had gone, so had the self-pity and the hospitalisation lure was just an embarrassing memory.

When the two detectives were about four yards away, one of them said, "Can we have a word with you, sir?" He was ginger-haired. I was pleased that at least even in my present state I rated a *sir*. I watched them close in on me and monitored them as they did to get a bead on whether they fancied me as the Durham escapee. I couldn't be definitive but there wasn't enough emergency about them to warrant that conclusion.

As they got near grabbing distance, I took off. I cut left into a road that ran parallel with the telephone kiosk road. "Stop!" one of them shouted. I had already dropped them. I just thought, "Save your breath for running arsehole, but it's no good saving it if you haven't the head to use it." I ran about thirty yards and turned right into a pedestrian thoroughfare leading up to a main road, which was full of traffic. I crossed the road and climbed over a fence on the opposite side that enclosed some school playing fields. I ran towards a concrete play-ground area adjoining the school buildings, past bicycle sheds and over another fence into some allotments. The turbo power surge was back again, but it was time to go to ground as by now the two dropped detectives would have radio'd up for help.

A boy and his father were working on their patch and looked at me with interest. I came out of the allotments into a street of small flat-fronted terrace houses; I slowed down to walk and looked round for a hidey hole. The place would be alive in a moment. Each pair of houses shared a wooden shed about as large as a small lavatory which stood on a tiny concrete area at the front. I loitered, looked carefully around, then went over to one of them, opened the top half-door and jumped in on top of the heap of coal inside. I closed the half-door behind me and leaned back against a shelf that had potted plants and gardening tools on it.

I waited and listened carefully but there was no sign that anyone who had seen me climbing in the shed. Then the silence was broken by the police cars screeching up and down the street and the adjoining area. After about a quarter of an hour it became quieter again. It was getting dark and I heard the jingle bells of an ice-cream van – at the end of October!

I reviewed my situation. If they connected the tramp with the escapee from Durham, the telephone box could have been alive with police; but Chester-le-Street was ten miles north of Durham. There was no edge to any of the detectives. If the first detective at the kiosk had fancied me as the escapee, he would have called up a bit more help than two walkers. I decided to go back and plot up for the 8 o'clock meet. I would pick up if there was a *ready-I* (ambush) around the kiosk and unless they had a Lee Evans (400 metres in 43.38s, Olympiad) in their ranks I would always get away. And if there was a ready-I or the car didn't show, I had my plan – go for broke, steal a car, break in somewhere, find some food, whatever it took. But they would have to catch me. I wasn't giving up.

I waited roughly an hour and a half before leaving the shed. I made my way back to the telephone kiosk. I approached it through the pedestrian thoroughfare. It looked deserted, but I knew that if they fancied the tramp was me they would have fingerprinted the telephone. I walked quickly round the box and checked it for powder – nothing. Then, I backed off to a side garden about twenty yards away where I could monitor the scene. I thought to myself that if you have to have the police hunting you, the farther north they come from the better. Eating ice cream in October can't be good for the brain cells.

After about ten minutes a police car drove up and a uniformed officer got out, walked past the box and onto the grass verge next to the wall that I used to sit on when I was waiting for a call. He glanced around, returned to the car and drove off. This wobbled me – they must have fancied the tramp was me, otherwise they would not be checking the kiosk. Yet the policeman's check was a desultory after-time affair. It had no emergency to it, so they must have assumed that I had taken off again. This was how I read it.

Two minutes later a black Morris Oxford pulled up beside the box but no-one got out. I thought it was a CID car. It was underneath the street light and I could see there were two men in it. A minute later, a man got out from the front passenger seat to walk to the telephone box. He looked round – he had a sheepskin coat on. I could see the curly white wool of the collar.

It was my man. I jumped over the wall of the little garden I was plotting up in and ran towards him. He looked towards me. "John?"

"Yeah, yeah," I said. He opened the back door and I got in. He went round the car and got into the front passenger seat and we moved off. They turned back and went up to the main road. I felt a marvellous sense of weakness and helplessness steal over me. No more decisions, no more risks; I was like a child again, cared for and protected. Most of all, I was now going to begin to live again.

The driver asked, "What took you so long? We were waiting there for a couple of minutes."

"Jean said the car was red. It's black. I only came out after I saw the sheepskin."

He laughed. "It is red, maroon, only it looks black under the fluorescent lights."

I told them quickly about the events of the last two hours and said that, on balance, it looked like they fancied I was in the area. They told me there had been no road blocks on the way up and they decided to steam straight back to London by the same route they had come up. I changed into some proper clothes and, most of all, shoes. We got rid of the stuff I'd been wearing. After about twenty-five miles we pulled into a cafe and I went into the washroom to clean up. I stared into the mirror at a gaunt, exhausted face with flat, sunken eyes – it was a burnt-out fanatic, not me.

I washed and went back to the car where they gave me a milk bottle filled with tea, which I drank as we drove along. Everything started to ache now and the drink also gave me stomach cramp. As soon as the cramp eased, we stopped at another cafe and this time they got me two bottles and some sandwiches. I ate in the car but they drove so fast that I kept getting nervous about the speed. It seemed dangerously reckless to me. When I voiced my concerns, they just laughed at me. I'd been in prison too long.

As we came nearer to London my excitement mounted at the feat I'd pulled off. We drove onto the North Circular at the bottom of Highgate Hill. "I've really made it now," I said. It made me feel warm and emotional – if I'd been on my own I might well have cried with the joy of it. I was on top of my mountain.

The two guys who picked me up in their car had never met me before and received nothing for doing it. If I had offered payment they would have been insulted. What can you say or do about people like that, except name your children after them? As for myself, I lost sixteen pounds in body weight and gained two years of freedom, during which I learned to love things I had forfeited before I even knew they existed.

Did I deserve it? I don't suppose so. I made a lot of mistakes, but life isn't a chess game. Luck protected me from my mistakes. Even now, when I dedicate a book I write "Be lucky". Anyway, our freedom, our ability to make our own lives, is always much smaller than we assume. But I didn't take my luck for granted – I used it well. During my two years of freedom I made more sense of my life than twenty years of imprisonment would have taught me.

For the professional and committed criminal, crime is a sort of blood sport played for real. It's not only a game and a business as, say, boxing can be, but also a way of life. A vocation really...not a worthy one but a vocation nonetheless. I came back to London in the knowledge that the only way I could stay free was by being a more successful criminal. The trouble was that on the way I'd lost belief in my vocation. It was just little things like the screw who gave me the slippers, Callaghan treating me as an equal, the decency of Greene, the treachery of Charlie, the way Wally helped me over the spikes, the students in Durham, Jean, the two guys who drove unpaid to collect an escapee they didn't even know...even the rat on the drainpipe. Some things you can't honour by being a criminal.

EPILOGUE

CHARLIE RICHARDSON served 17 years and was released in 1984. In 1981, he walked out of an open prison over being refused parole, giving himself up 9 months later. In 1993 he published *My Manor*, a book that was written by an ex-journalist, in which he exposed the conspiracy that was behind his conviction. In 2001, a company called Midas Films offered investors a stake in a proposed film based on his life. A *Guardian* article ("Made to look a right Charlie") in November 2001 noted that the investors had been subjected to "not physical but fiscal torture". Charlie, as the trial judge observed in 1966, still remains "a disgrace to society". Eventually, Midas did produce Charlie (2003) but it went lead not gold at the box office.

EDDIE RICHARDSON served nearly 10 years and was living quietly with his family until his brother was released. Towards the end of his own sentence, Charlie had been totting up the amount of money being made in the drug trade. He said to Eddie, "They are making millions, millions. We've got to have some of it." In 1990, Eddie was sentenced to 25 years for conspiracy to smuggle cocaine worth millions into the UK. The last time he spoke to his brother was soon after he started this sentence in Whitemoor Prison. Eddie said, "You've ruined my life." Warders had to haul him off Charlie. He served 11 years and was paroled in 2001. He still doesn't talk to Charlie.

ROY HALL served just over 6 years and was released in 1972. He did not inherit the scrap metal yard that Charlie had promised him but he worked in the trade and never went back to prison.

EPILOGUE

TONY DUNFORD served 22 years of his life sentence. He was awarded a double first in philosophy while he served it. When he was released in 1985, he worked as a scaffolder, then was eventually offered a lectureship in the Bristol area. He has never re-offended.

TONY LAWRENCE was released in 1977 after serving 9 years. He returned to his old manor, Fulham, where he faded into obscurity.

JOHN STRAFFEN is still in prison. He has been there longer than any other serving prisoner. He was jailed in 1952 and in 2004 at the age of 74 he had served 52 years. He has been told that he will die in prison.

TONY ***KARATE*** **CREAMER** was released after 12 years, in 1978. Nothing is known about him but it seems that he did not re-offend.

WALLY PROBYN served 10 years of his sentence and was released in 1975. He dabbled in Scientology, then became involved in running a hostel for battered wives. On May 25, 1995, he was jailed for four years for indecency offences, involving a young girl and the distribution of pornographic photographs. His counsel described him as a "broken man" and lacking the will to live. The offences inovolved two charges of taking indecent photographs of a child under 16, two indecent assaults and possessing indecent photographs. The Old Bailey judge told him: "No-one who has listened to this case could help but be disgusted at the low level to which you sank." His counsel said: "He felt deep shame in relation to these offences and talked about the label he would carry to his grave. He now lacks the will to live. He has been completely alienated from his family and those who know him."

ADAM FAITH, the actor who played Probyn in the film *McVicar*, died March 8th 2003. He was on the road in his latest show with a 21-year-old groupie. They returned to his hotel room in Stoke-on-Trent and switched on Channel Five, he said to her, "Channel Five is all shit isn't it? It's a waste of space." Then he suffered a fatal heart attack.

JOHN McVICAR

People who read this book often ask why I don't include myself in the epilogue. I suppose I should but I don't really know what to say. Instead I have decided to repeat what I wrote in my instructions to counsel, which were read by the trial judge, when I appeared at the Old Bailey in 1971 on robbery and firearm charges committed while I was an escapee from Durham:

"I don't serve my time like a criminal anymore. I don't curry favour with prison staff but I am not disruptive nor will I try to escape again. I will use my time to study and re-educate myself, to pick up where I left off at Grammar School. That is what I shall do. When I am released I will work, hopefully, using the fruits of my prison studies."

That's what I did.

PART TWO:

MITIGATION PLEA

Introduction

'Mitigation Plea' like 'Escape' was written in my cell at Brixton Prison after I had been recaptured in November 1970. It was written with no less intent than 'Escape' but my goal was nothing to do with money and all to do with ensuring that I did not go to prison for life on firearms' charges. I had been captured with an arsenal of guns that had only one purpose: armed robbery. My existing sentence at this time was 23 years and what I wanted to avoid at all costs was a judge just deciding enough is enough and sending me down for life. Yet the target of 'Mitigation Plea' was not so much the trial judge as my barrister, Malcolm Morris QC. It was him I had to convince that I would never return to crime.

Morris was a distinguished silk whose poor health was all that had stopped him being appointed to the High Court. Nonetheless, he had that kind of standing at the bar. From my point of view, he was a good barrister in that he knew the law, but what made him a great barrister was that he not only knew the judges but also was seen by them as an equal.

I needed a barrister who not only would plead my cause in chambers with the sentencing judge but also whose personal judgement would be respected and acted on. Morris was perfect for that and my choice was helped by the fact that we had got on well during the previous trial. However, I knew that if he was going to pull the all strings and pull out all the stops, too, I had to impress him with my change of direction. And I knew the only way I could do that was through the written word.

Judges and senior barristers are intellectuals. They live professionally by the reasoned argument, especially the written word. In the rough and tumble of overseeing the criminal justice system judges are often intellectually dishonest. As long as they think the Appeal Court will not strike them down, they will rule against the weight of the precedents; they will direct a trial against the grain of the evidence; if they think the jury is getting it wrong, they will try to bring home the verdict in their summing up. Nonetheless, I knew that if someone like me came in from the cold and makes a strong case for leniency they would give him a break. If they got it wrong with me, it wouldn't matter. I was a nonentity who, if he reneged on his commitment, would hurt himself and his immediate family far more than he would society.

My task was to explain why I had become a criminal and do it in such a persuasive way that the analysis would demonstrate that it was unlikely I would offend again. However calculating, opportunistic, even cynical this sounds, the fact is I had decided to give up crime. But it was no good just proclaiming it, I had to convince the people who would decide my fate that this was so.

I took as my model *De Profundis*, which is what Oscar Wilde called his testament written in Reading Jail in 1897. I have read *De Profundis* more times than Osama bin Laden has the Koran. In my opinion, although it is only essay length, it is **the** prison book. Prisoner reformers never mention or read it because, while it is about change, it is not about the kind of programmable change that therapists want to be funded to implement. Prisoner counsellors, treaters and therapists did not exist in Wilde's day but he would have scorned these people with as much venom as he did those who punish in the name of reform.

> 'Never attempt to reform a man... To punish a man for wrong-doing with a view to his reformation is the most lamentable mistake it is possible to commit. If he has any soul at all, such a procedure is calculated to make him ten times worse than before. It is the sign of a noble nature to refuse to be broken by force (Wilde).'

My task, then, was to show myself to Morris as a changed man by writing my own knockdown *De Profundis.* All these years later, I cringe at my ambition to write even a third-rate version. But I was encouraged by the fact that I had also served time in Reading Prison. When I went there it was a Punishment Borstal whose only treatment was "a fucking good kicking". Eventually it was closed down because of this. I hated the place and the staff that ran it. However, I took a perverse delight in the way the regime exposed the lies and contradictions of the

Borstal branch of the penal system.

Borstal Training was only given to youths, aged 16 to 21, who were considered more suitable for training and reform rather than a punitive prison sentence. The whole idea was a sham. The vocational training itself was utterly worthless, the regimes were often more punitive than a prison's and, worst of all, the concept itself was unjust.

The Borstal Training sentence was of a duration of 9 months to three years. Thus it was an indeterminate sentence, the length of which depended upon how staff assessed the prisoner's response to training. Rehabilitation tends to go hand-in-hand with an indeterminate sentence because only when the rehabilitators have some control over when a prisoner is discharged will those being treated collude with the regime.

What a Borstal sentence did, though, was break a central tenet of justice: that the severity of the sentence should reflect the gravity of the crime. Once a sentencing system breaches this higher order claim of justice, however enlighted or civilized its lower order tenets, it must and always does cause more harm to society than would otherwise be the case.

The consequence of the Borstal system being more unjust than its prison counterpart was to produce more rebels. Given that many Borstal Boys knew they would serve less time in better conditions, if they had been sentenced to imprisonment, it was no wonder some rebelled. The purpose of Reading Prison when it was a Punishment Borstal was to terrorise these rebels back into line. The regime at Reading's Punishment Borstal was far more violent than the equivalent in an ordinary prison. Inevitably, the effect of this was to affirm and reinforce criminality.

Sadly for me and the taxpayers who footed the bill for my criminal antics, my hatred of the place blinded me to the way it made me a worse criminal. I still carry residues of my hatred for the place, so that even forty years later, when I look at the football results, I get a little buzz if Reading Football Club lose!

De Profundis was written over three months in 1897 in the form of a symbolic love letter to his catamite, Lord Alfred 'Bosie' Douglas, whose father brought about Wilde's downfall and the 2 years hard labour that went with it. It is a rambling, disjointed, brilliant, lyrical but always profound composition. The truth it clarifies is intrinsic to the human condition. What lies at its heart is how Wilde as an artist tackled what humans have always done when they have become dissatisfied with their lives. They put themselves under the microscope; they conduct a stocktake of their character; they analyse themselves.

There is nothing unusual in this. Nor is there anything unusual in the circumstances in which Wilde did it. We all have problems but, when one is caught up in the hurly-burly of life, the tendency is to live with them and get on with things as best one can. Generally people only reflect upon themselves and the life they are living when, first, they are overwhelmed by some tragic event and, second, they have time to think. The classic conditions that provoke self-examination are serious illness; death of a lover, parent or child; imprisonment; public disgrace or failure.

Wilde's account of this process is inspiring because it springs from the best in the human condition. It is not based upon religion or social science and its only ideological edge is life as art. His aesthetic of ethical individualism is intelligent, compassionate, discerning, tolerant...

DeProfundis is packed with ideas and insight – every time I re-read it I underline fresh passages – but what always takes me back to it is its simple humanity. We all live a life and how we live it shapes how we are. The catch with this iron law is that how we are determines how we tune into the world. If we don't live well, whatever our successes, riches or fame, we cannot experience life well.

The heart-wrenching tragedy of Wilde is that he saw how to direct 'the ethical evolution of one's character' but spells in Wandsworth and Reading prisons had broken his body and spirit – he could not follow what he understood and believed in. At the time he wrote *De Profundis*, though, he did not know this. Instead he was optimistic that his new insights would be realised in his art and in his sensibilities: 'I hope to live long enough and to produce work of such a character that I shall be able at the end of my days to say, "Yes, this is just where the artistic life leads a man!"'

Ignorant that he would fail, he nevertheless observes how tragic it is that so few people even try to master their lives. 'Most people are other people,' he observes. 'Their thoughts are someone else's opinion, their lives a mimicry, their passions a quotation... The intellectual and emotional life of ordinary people is a very contemptible affair. Just as they borrow their ideas from a sort of circulating library of thought...so they always try to get their emotions on credit, or refuse to pay the bill when it comes in.' The road back from ugliness and ignobility, though, means going back up the same road that we went down: this time living it well, not badly.

Wilde offers no escape from the brute fact that the way we live our lives so we are, although there are now far more agencies offering crutches that weaken the will rather than strengthen it than there were in his day. As he would have despised those who want to treat criminals, so he would have despised all the therapists who have appointed themselves experts in dealing with such moral problems as drug addiction, obesity, sexual perversion, bullying, unhappiness…

He would also have been disgusted with the way these people have usurped our cultural remedies for dealing with these problems, put a pseudo-scientific spin on what they have hijacked, then in the name of science promoted themselves as experts in curing these ills.

As he describes in *De Profundis*, Wilde looked at himself when he was in prison; when I was on the run from my 23 year sentence, I did too, albeit in a cursory fashion. Being on the run from a 23 year jail sentence was certainly better than serving it. Nonetheless, I was acutely aware how betrayal, a mistake, just chance could see me back serving longer or just dead from a shoot-out with the police. At 29 years old, I was on the edge, living a day at a time, but my conditions were conducive to reflection, even introspection.

I was doing what I could to amass enough money from crime to have a stab at starting a new life abroad, while aware of the long odds on that coming off. Given that I was cooped up in a flat with very little contact with anyone, I had a lot of time on my hands. About the only people I saw regularly were my son and his mother.

One afternoon, I was watching my son playing around at the side of the bed on which I was sprawled. He was five, happy, secure and blissfully unaware of the fragility of our family life. The imagination can play funny tricks when one is under pressure and feeling guilty. Suddenly in my mind's eye I saw myself as a child in him – in place of him I literally saw myself as I was at his age, looking like I did and wearing the clothes that I wore then. I also felt the shock of the ugliness I had wrought from such charm, innocence and potential. This timeshift lasted five seconds or so, then, as reality re-asserted itself, the interpretation of what it meant kicked in. One didn't need the mind of Sigmund Freud or, for that matter, Oscar Wilde, to appreciate what my subconscious was telling me.

I am not prone to visions, so this experience had a formidable impact on me. I will never forget it but, over the following year or so, it exerted a powerful influence on me and it seeded a cold, objective self-examination of myself and how I had lived.

Towards the end of my two years at large I realised that my earlier hopes of securing enough money to go abroad were a pipe dream and the inevitability of capture or death came to claim my mind. It was in this doom-laden limbo that I resolved that if I lived I would never try to escape again or return to crime. It was the least I could do to make some kind of amends.

'Mitigation Plea' is just a fleshing out of this earlier analysis. It is a very cold, naked, detached document, which I am sometimes tempted just to drop from this book. It does not belong with 'Escape' but it was bolted onto it in 1974 and I always baulk at uncoupling it.

At the time, though, it did the trick of influencing who it was aimed at influencing. The sentencing judge called it "this very moving document". Whether he actually read it is a moot point but I knew that

Malcolm Morris had briefed him on it in chambers since Morris indicated before sentence that I must expect "some extra time" on my sentence. A modest increment. He also assured me that I would not get life imprisonment.

Nine months after re-capture, I got another three years, which on the scale of things mattered neither here nor there.

On the 30th Anniversary of this book (2004), I don't notice any less interest in the subject of crime and punishment. The debate still rages, although it waxes and wanes in its intesity. At the moment, it is waxing and there also seems to be a shift away from the concept of rehabilitation as the guiding principle of the criminal justice system towards one of just deserts or retribution. Nonetheless, the rehabilitationists still occupy the high moral ground.

Yet I stopped contributing to the debate some years ago because the rehabilitationists were ideologically committed and their cause was aided and abetted by a sympathetic media elite. They also cheated in their arguments, and still do.

People with a stake in the prisoner-reform industry ignore the fact that personal responsibility lies at the heart of our criminal justice system. Indeed, they seem ignorant of how personal freedom and being held to account for the choices one makes are virtually cornerstones of capitalist democracy. But personal responsibility and being held to account are certainly fundamental in the first two phases that an offender must go through before he is delivered for rehabilitation to the social engineers of prison.

During investigation and trial, the suspect or the

accused is deemed responsible for his actions. The prison warders who feed, water, bed and exercise the livestock take a similar view but not so the reformers and rehabilitators. Their existence is predicated on the prisoner needing help to reform or address his offending behaviour and, while their activities are just rhetoric, it is a foolhardy inmate who in the era of parole does not pay lip service to their rehab courses.

I always think of the concept of rehabilitation as being like the one of heaven. We might all wish such a place as heaven existed, we might all agree that it would be a good place and we can all imagine what it might be like. However, no critical thinker lets wishful thinking lead him into magical thinking. No critical thinker assumes that heaven exists.

A lot of people, though, do assume that heaven exists. Indeed, there are massive organisations that foster and encourage such beliefs. They run courses on how to get to heaven and meet a skygod. They have rituals, tests and man the entrance gates that heaven-seekers have to go through to earn their ticket.

Some cynical heavenists doubtless admit in the privacy of their own mind that they are trafficking in delusion. They probably comfort themselves with the rationalisation that it comforts those in distress and gives hope to the hopeless. Yet it is a monstrous thing to earn your livelihood by encouraging people to sell out the only life they have for a delusion.

While rehabilitation and heaven are both concepts of magical thinking, more reality checks can be brought to bear on the former. After all, asking the spirits in the sky about heaven requires entering the same realm that we are checking out. We can, however, look at the results of the courses run by rehabilitationists. We can examine whether the claims they make stand up. They don't. There is no systematic relationship between a form of rehabilitation and reduced rates of re-offending.

In fact, the most successful form of response to crime is just plain just deserts. That is the best we can do. However, cynical rehabilitationists probably say, like their heavenist counterparts, that rehab courses don't do any harm and, in fact, do some good in that they keep convicts and warders busy, even raise their morale. Yet, when you try to do more than you can, you invariably hamper and impede achieving what is possible. Rehabilitationists corrupt justice and damage lives, not in such a heinous way as heavenists, but sufficiently to attract the disdain and ridicule of all critical thinkers.

I have hacked around journalism for 25 years and every day I remind myself – *think critically*. For all its guttersnipe image, journalism engages in the daily, ongoing interpretation of social reality for others who are too busy or distant from the issues to do it themselves. If I am being paid to witter on about, say, crime and punishment, then I have certain obligations to do it responsibly. Social truths may be contingent and relative but, aside from the resources we draw on to understand the world, we are all still engaged in the reproduction of and contribution to social reality. We do that with our supply of definitions of the situation.

A journalist who misinterprets the world for others, therefore, is supplying them with inferior or just plain bad tools for living. That is how lives are corrupted. When people act on the basis of wishful or magical thinking or misinformation, then their intentions will be thwarted, their own lives damaged and probably those of others around them. A responsible journalist, then, is honour-bound to interpret the world critically and accurately in terms of what is known.

Rehabilitationists never think critically... if they did they wouldn't be rehabilitationists. Nonetheless, despite my retirement from the fray, people still occasionally ask why I changed and my reply is always the same. "Just as I chose to commit crime when I was young, so when I was older I chose not to. The only difference between the two choices was the circumstances." Of course, this is a flip answer that hides more than it reveals. But we all get older and probably the most valuable compensation for doing so is to get wiser. Some of us only do so by learning from our mistakes. I guess I am one of them, but in the end it worked. Moreover, despite the pains inflicted by the mistakes, I am more than compensated by the knowledge that my change was directed by my own free will.

I may have written my 'Mitigation Plea' for the purpose of reducing my sentence but I also had the vague hope that others tempted to follow my path might, in reading it, learn from my mistakes without making them.

John McVicar, 2004.

MITIGATION PLEA, 1971

For Malcolm Morris QC:

I have already served ten years in prison and even on an optimistic count I must serve another ten years of my current sentence before I can realistically hope to be paroled. No one can waste so much of the past and forfeit so much of the future as I have without thinking deeply about the reasons for what is on anyone's count a travesty of a life. I know what has happened in my life and I think I also know the reasons for it. This document is a summary of that knowledge: an account of how I let my criminality blight a life that once held so much promise.

It is not intended as an excuse or even a defence; it is merely intended to be true.

John, three years; and Janice one year

Diane McVicar, Hyde Park Piazza 1984.

The early years

I was born in March 1940, during the London blitz. My earliest memories are associated with shelters and doodlebugs, but I was never frightened by the war and I know it had no traumatic effect on me. My sister, Janice, was born two years after me. My parents had no more children.

My father was excused from armed service because of ill health and he worked out the war years in the railway yards. He was an enterprising man who first ran a newspaper stall near East Ham underground station, then bought a corner shop in a busy side road that ran up to the same station. I suspect that his enterprising spirit was also connected with his avoidance of the draft. The main trade of the shop was newspapers and tobacco but he also stocked groceries and confectionery. We all lived in the rooms at the back of the shop and this was my home until I received my first prison sentence at 16.

I have no memories of my father during the war years, simply a vague impression of him being around. The main feature of his life was the long and exhausting hours he worked: he rose at 6 am and did not finish until 7 pm. He had a two-hour lunch break and, on Sunday, he closed the shop at 1 pm. Running the shop ruled his life.

I know very little about his background, except that he was of Scottish extraction. He never spoke about himself; he was a reserved, solitary, even morose man who drank. Yet he married a woman who was warm, emotional, sociable. It made a bad match, but they had two children before realising it and never separated in spite of the recurrent crises over his drinking. Mine and my sister's upbringing took place against the background of their constant arguments, rows and occasional fights. As parents, my mother was loving and indulgent, my father cold and uncommunicative – but he was never cruel or arbitrarily violent with either me or my sister.

I entered Infants' School in the autumn of 1945. The most significant thing that I felt towards my father at that time was indifference. I don't think I was, as yet, aware of his drinking, but certainly his hostility to my mother and his self-imposed exile in the shop hindered my forming a normal bond of identification with him. The absence of a father to model myself on did not interfere with my defining myself as a boy and adopting standards that I saw as appropriate. Although I loved my mother intensely, I knew that she was a woman and not a role model.

However, it wasn't merely that I didn't identify with my father, I did not model myself on any adult male. So the usual process by which a child absorbs the values of his society passed me by. Instead, my models were drawn from the society of my peers, mainly other – often older – street kids. Of course, all boys pick up some of this but in my case it was unbalanced. I was all street kid. Given my father's drinking and damaged character, it was probably good for the stability of my own personality that I didn't identify with him but the kind of environment that I grew up in deposited its own destructive time-bombs.

The first ambition I can remember having was to be the best fighter in the Infants' School. In Primary School this was supplemented by an obsession with sport and any other activity which carried prestige in the eyes of other boys. I suppose that the admiration I won in this way compensated for the lack of admiration from my father. Unfortunately, my competitiveness and my need to dominate my companions became the basis of my own self-esteem. I was a little tearaway who only felt good about himself when he proved that he was tough by beating up or lording it over other boys.

I was a naturally physical child who was born with a lot of advantages in terms of strength, speed and endurance, which served me well in sport and in enduring the discipline and criticism of teachers. At home I had the love of an adoring mother; my indifferent, largely absent father hardly intruded in my life, while at school I was good at everything kids celebrate in the playground. I was constantly in trouble with teachers but, as I was not delinquent, it never went any further. I was a stable, secure kid and by my own standards during my years at Primary School very successful.

But schooling is intended to equip the future adult for a socially-approved role in life and, in this respect, the values I had embraced were loaded towards the anti-social. I believed not only that fighting was the best method of settling any dispute but also that courage and success in showing aggression provided the only true basis for self-esteem. I never believed in authority, which in practice meant I never invoked authority to settle a dispute. More importantly I never obeyed authority unless I wanted to or the consequences of disobedience were not worth the candle.

Of course, a lot of boys grow up with similar attitudes but in my case it was more extreme than most. So by the time I left Primary School, my character was already developing along machismo lines that, while they did not lead inexorably to crime, did make it a possible destination. Nevertheless, as I was not a disturbed child and as my victims were confined to the playground, I was not anti-social in a delinquent sense. I never stole anything or vandalised property or even bunked off school. I was just a little playground Al Capone.

Some boys who are blooded in this kind of outlook find law-abiding work. Professional sport is obviously one outlet, the armed forces or the police service another, but the law-abiding pickings are pretty lean. Then there is crime. Given my attitude towards authority, an all-seeing betting man would have made crime odds on.

By the age of 6 or 7, I was already an enthusiastic member of the street gang where I must have absorbed my values subconsciously from the older boys that I admired. It was a seamless process. I was an extrovert and adaptable child on the rebound from my mother's femininity and unattached to any adult male. All unsupervised working-class boys settle their disputes and pecking order by fighting. I quickly adopted the test of fighting as the fairest means of settling conflicts, the truest measure of prestige and the foundation of self-esteem. In fact, the germs of these values must have been implanted in me even before I went to school, because I can distinctly remember that my only worry when I first went was whether I would make it as a fighter. But even then it was all very sporting. I wanted to win without cheating and I certainly never really hurt another child.

I can't place when I first knew that my father drank and that this was a bad thing, but I can remember him taking me and my sister to a Christmas pantomime at the East End Palace when I was five or six. It had been snowing and though the pavements were clean, snow was piled in the gutters. The theatre was only at the top of our street and as we approached it my father slipped and fell behind a car parked by the kerb. A couple who had been coming towards us, and had perhaps forced my father onto the slippery edge of the pavement, went to his assistance.

My sister and I were beside him as he pulled himself up on the bumper of the car but, as the couple came closer, the woman recoiled and said scornfully and indignantly, "He's drunk." In asides to her husband, she banged on about the iniquity of a drunkard being in charge of two small children.

I knew what being drunk meant and I was not surprised or shocked at the word being applied to my father. I felt sorry for him, but even that reaction had very little filial content to it.

Later on we got used to him being a drunk. When we were still small, he would sometimes take us out on Sunday afternoons, which was the only time he was not in the shop. We used to dread these outings. Inevitably he would stop at a pub and, after he had supplied us with crisps and lemonade, we would look through the door and see him at the bar downing shorts, totally oblivious to the jostling, chattering Sunday crowd around him. Except for some financial crisis or illness, forcing him on the wagon, he drank every day of his life.

I don't know why he drank. He was never the typical friendly, rollicking drunkard, just a more isolated and rigid version of his normal self. When I was about seven my mother moved him out of her bedroom and, though I never understood the significance of it, as far as I knew, they never slept together again. He had a lonely, miserable life. Yet, he always worked, was scrupulously honest and what problems he had were contained within his family where they exacted their own price.

After I began to go to school my communication with my father was almost entirely restricted to asking him for something – either money or the things that money will buy. But I had no affection for him and, while I never hated him, his drunkenness and the grief he gave my mother gave me an excuse for pretending that I did. I describe these matters, not to suggest that they had any harmful effect on me, but to illustrate how impossible it was for my father to influence me.

With my mother things were entirely different. I was as close and affectionate to her as she was devoted and loving to me. I was fiercely proud of her. But I can see now that she compensated for the emotional poverty of her life by making a career out of her children. As we grew older, besides being the beneficiaries of her devotion, we also became the sympathetic audience to her martyrdom in enduring the pains of her marriage.

No doubt at the beginning we were the spoils over which she and my father fought, but his drunkenness disqualified him from the battle and, early on, he withdrew to the consolation of the bottle. My mother was openly contemptuous of "him", who was always in the shop and more often than not drunk. He reciprocated with a quiet sarcasm when we carried messages between them. Both my sister and I would openly express our hatred of him in his absence and he must have known, although we were not sophisticated enough to realise that. For all his limitations, he was an intelligent and worldly man who would have picked up on our feelings towards him. My mother had won a cruel victory in her marital war. Yet she was under the intense and bewildering pressure of trying to cope with a problem she didn't understand. As a naturally sociable woman, it also marooned her on a desert island of shame. Responsible for two children, she did what she could. Her only alternatives were to desert us all or to sink into irreversible despair. She did neither; she stayed with it.

When I was arrested this last time, Detective Chief Inspector Morrison who led the manhunt for me came into my cell to tell me that my mother had been on the phone. I showed my embarrassment as I knew she would have gone on and on about how I was a good boy. I had just been two years on the run from a 23 year jail sentence with a £10,000 dead or alive reward on my head but to my mother I was still her little darling. He said, quizzically, "She's a neurotic, isn't she, John?" It wasn't said offensively, he was genuinely puzzled.

I replied, "Anyone would be neurotic with two children like me and my sister." I didn't add that we were the second generation of problems that she had shouldered. She was over-wrought – she had borne too much worry and anxiety and it showed. But she had been driven into this condition by insoluble problems that were never of her own making. It was Herculean the way she kept going, always picking up everyone's pieces before she picked up her own.

I was eighteen, in prison and already a committed, full-time criminal when my father died. Soon after, my sister became a casualty of my own way of life. She became a barbiturate addict and was convicted of drug offences. On the way, she had two daughters and my mother has been the only lasting and effective parent they have known. Just as she never deserted my father or myself or my sister, so she would never abandon her two grandchildren.

She always showed astonishing courage and resilience in protecting her family against the worst consequences of their failings. I am saying this because the last thing she deserves is the objectivity of this document. Perhaps the saddest thing about my present predicament is that if, as a child, I had felt the same sense of awe that I do now for her courage, thrift, loyalty and decency I could never have become a criminal

Whatever time was left over from competing for ascendancy among my companions, I spent practising and performing at football, boxing, swimming, cricket, athletics and so on. I was obsessed with sport, and it is notable that the roles I adopted in sport were always the hostile, aggressive and dominating ones. At football I was a forward; at cricket a fast bowler; I saw the essence of athletics in the long, gruelling races; and my style as a boxer owed little to the art of self-defence. And whatever the sport, I was above all a competitor. To some extent my sporting prowess absolved me from some of the punishment from teachers for my classroom antics. Nonetheless, these patterns of behaviour – empire-building in the playground, disobedience to authority, aggressiveness in sport – were the main themes of my social development. Their criteria of excellence were my standards of self-esteem.

Intellectually, things were more complicated. To be clever was an advantage, but working hard at school was a definite minus in the status stakes among my peer-group. But in these matters my mother was an influence. She had encouraged me to read at an early age and had taught me to love books and feel the fascination of learning. So I steered a middle course and though my schoolwork was never as good as it could have been, it passed muster.

At home there were none of the temptations for earning peer group awe by classroom disobedience or the scope for domination offered by the playground. I bullied my sister – she was a girl. But my father had opted out of my upbringing. Virtually isolated in the shop, his function was reduced for all practical purposes to that of a distant and ultimate sanction.

I depended on my mother for emotional warmth and security, which she supplied in abundance, but I rejected her control because she was a woman. Though I loved her and turned to her in distress, I did not accept her discipline or her guidance in spheres of activity that I regarded as male preserves. The independence she fostered in me only aggravated the problem. Of course, I now know that much of what I am describing is very common in lower-class boys raised in matriarchal households.

All these influences were inculcating attitudes and values in me that, while not critical in my criminal career, were necessary conditions and predisposing factors for when, in my teens, circumstances threw up the option of living by crime.

My role as the school tough was consolidated pretty well during my Primary School days, and I put quite a lot of work into maintaining the integrity of my position. Action was necessary not only against challengers to my playground fiefdom but even against anyone who called me names. I was particularly sensitive to insults and punishing offenders involved me in a good deal of trouble with the headmaster. But no matter how often I was caned, I never accepted that I could not hit any boy who insulted me. The headmaster himself was not an enthusiastic caner. Instead, he preferred to "talk" to persistent rule-breakers. On one occasion he had me in his office at the top of the school for whacking some kid and "talked" to me.

He used the distress I was causing my mother to make me feel guilty. It was not the sort of school for a Parent-Teacher Association, so the fact that he even knew my mother was in itself ominous. As he made me feel the unhappiness my antics were causing her, I sobbed my heart out, which was something that no end of caning had achieved. Needless to say, it did not make me change my ways.

In my last year, when I was crowned king of the playground, I was also deposed – ironically enough by a policeman's son. He was a friend of mine, but got sick of my domineering behaviour and beat me in a straight fight from which the referee, also a friend, allowed me to retire because of a cut. I went home shattered and was greeted by a hysterical mother who could not have understood in a thousand years where the pain really was. What woman could? It was my first really traumatic experience. I had lost my title and I felt an immense sense of unworthiness in my failure to epitomise the values that I subscribed to.

Perhaps I learned the fear of defeat; perhaps I learned to be more politic in my power play; perhaps I learned that there is no disgrace in losing when you have done your best… But whatever lessons I learned, they were not going to deliver me from machismo.

Although I was a long way from being a criminal, there were certain aspects of crime that fascinated me. By the time I was eleven, I was reading library books and one in particular absorbed me completely. It was a novel called *Little Caesar* by W. F. Burnett, which was about a racketeer whose character was based upon Al Capone. While the novel's main character was a repulsive Charlie Richardson type, I was enthralled with the way in which he built up his power and empire. It made such an impact on me that years later, when I was nineteen, I came across it again and reread it eagerly.

As I did so I was kept wondering why it'd had such an impact on me at eleven and I read on to the end, searching for something in it that would explain my first reaction. But at nineteen it was a dud. I could not appreciate then that it was too badly written to grab me emotionally in my late teens in the same way it had in my pre-teens. Nonetheless, this book completely absorbed me when I was a child.

I was also an eager reader of a comic called *The Hotspur*. It consisted of serials intended to appeal to the early teenage group. But of all the many stories I must have read and enjoyed in it, I can only remember one. It was about a rogue cowboy who was being hunted down for a murder committed under very extenuating circumstances. He was brave and lived by his own code with great honesty and integrity. I identified completely with this character. His adventures thrilled and fascinated me. In the final episode when he was killed, sacrificing his life for the marshal who was hunting him down, I mourned his passing as much as the death of my cat, Fluffy. But this was not the only reading that enthralled me; at about the same time I read *Wuthering Heights*.

It was probably my passion for books that enabled me to pass the 11+ and go to a Grammar School in the Mile End called Coopers' Company School. The exams at the end of the first term showed how much I was out of my depth academically. Out of the first-year pupils, I came well down in the middle and I was placed in the second of the three first-year forms. This made me feel inadequate not only because of my poor performance but also because I was confused and depressed by my failure to grasp the new subjects. I was galvanised into working hard. I forced myself to master my lessons and at the end of the year I came out top of my class and about eighth or ninth in the whole year.

I was determined to do well and for the only time in my schooldays I showed the same determination and competitiveness in academic work that I did in sport. I became so competitive that when I was awarded a miserable 20% for Art – my weakest subject – I cried. I brooded for ages over this as art was not a subject I could learn. Another success in my first year at Grammar School was making the semi-finals of a handicap chess competition. My father had taught me to play when I was eight and I went on to study the game, which gave me a massive edge. It was tremendously gratifying to be sought out by hulking sixth-formers and ordered over to the chess room where I then proceeded to wipe them off the board.

Predictably I was also a hot-shot at sport, where I had already served my apprenticeship. When I look back now from the wrong end of a 23 year jail sentence at my first year at Coopers, the unfulfilled promise of it depresses me more than anything in my schooldays. If I had stayed with my studies, I could have gone on to university...well, at least been a contender. Although I kept up my chess and sport, the end of that year marked the beginning of a slow decline in my academic performance. I lost my drive and lessons and exams gradually became obstacles to circumvent with as little effort as possible.

Around this time, when I was twelve, my father came to watch me box – the only time he ever watched me do anything. Most of the time he was working, but this evening he attended a boxing card at Fairbairn House, a youth club in Canning Town. When my bout was over and I was changing, a friend came up to me and said, "Your dad asked me to tell you to go home alone as he had to go somewhere."

My mother condemned him bitterly, "The pig couldn't wait to have a drink." I didn't argue with her. But I had glimpsed him in the crowd, his eyes shining with pride. A child can't understand the craving for drink – perhaps only an addict can – but I knew that my mother's condemnation was harsh. I think he'd tried to get closer to me, but he was too out of practice and nothing changed.

I drifted on, my work gradually deteriorating, but not irretrievably so, until I reached puberty. I told myself that if I wanted to I could cut the academic mustard – after all, I had in the first year – but between 11 and 14 I was doing as little as I could get away with.

Disobedience in class was no longer a status symbol, so I just sloped by as a reluctant student rather than a disruptive influence.

My school was some distance from my neighbourhood and my friendships with my Primary School friends had fallen by the way, so I didn't have any street cronies to mix with after classes. Most of my social activities were school-centred. Sport and, oddly enough, chess monopolised most of my leisure hours. I won an Essex chess championship when I was thirteen and became a member of the school chess team when still fairly young.

My Primary School attitudes were dormant really since they certainly had not been supplanted by the Grammar School ethos. I still tried to dominate my peers but fighting did not have the potency it had had at Primary School. Even my boxing was not seen as especially admirable. My self-esteem was still rooted in being a tough guy but apart from sport I did not really have any way of being tough. Yet juvenile delinquency had no appeal; this was for misfits and inadequates. The absence of a socially approved role model with whom I could identify and whose authority I could accept had left me a lop-sided teenager, intellectually precocious, but callow, socially egocentric and emotionally crude rather than unstable.

Apart from a few sporting fantasies, I had no real ambitions about what I would do after I left school. I certainly did not want to stay and study for A levels and university. I had begun cheating in exams – not to do well, just to get by. I was in a classic adolescent drift, without focus or direction. Puberty changed all that and provided the soil in which all the seeds of machismo could come to fruition.

At about fourteen and a half, in my new male body, I decided I wanted to be an adult and do the things that adults do. Especially sex. I started to smoke, pestered my parents for smart adult clothes and rejected the manner and habits of my schoolmates with a vengeance. Classes and lessons became "stupid", a waste of time. I used to have self-pitying day-dreams about being paralysed from the waist down before I had ever had intercourse; it was the most miserable fate that I could imagine. I was not involved in any social activities in which I mixed with girls: school, youth clubs, friends, were all exclusively male. I started attending the local ice rink in the company of a slightly older friend from my Primary School days; from this I quickly progressed to local dance halls and hanging about milkshake bars. These were the places where I might pick up girls – this became the focal point of my life and everything else fell by the wayside.

My schoolwork suffered, and though I managed to limp along on my wits, by my fifteenth birthday I had more or less dropped out. I didn't even bother to cheat at exams. My sporting interests also waned but sport was still prestigious and I kept my hand in. My pursuit of sex pushed me into an entirely different social circle: youngsters who were older, working, but in dead-end jobs, uneducated and just out for a good time. They let me into their circle because in the ways that mattered to them I was mature for my age. I was quite tough, I had my wits about me and I had enough money sponged off my parents to pay my way.

Of course, things didn't stop there. I graduated to the snooker hall and the public house and, as I established myself on the fringe of this kind of world, I became both fascinated and challenged by it. Its inhabitants appealed to me: their rakishness, their flamboyant clothes, their tough, self-reliant manner, their rejection of conventional stances to sex and money. I was mesmerised by the desire to become a player in this world. I unconsciously modelled myself on the more successful representatives of this new society, which in fact was a vamped-up version of my old playground jungle.

The summer of 1955, when I was fifteen, was spent almost exclusively in the snooker hall and, by then, I played well enough to gamble on my skills. It is often noted that skill at snooker is the mark of a misspent youth. I can still pot a mean black. At school I became uncooperative and insolent, flouting the rules regarding clothes and hairstyle. Secure in the simplistic values of my new powerbase, I became a disruptive and subversive element. I was banned from class by some of the more sensitive teachers and more or less rejected all the benefits of education.

I started going up to the West End to the all-night record clubs; it was after one such all-night outing, after I had taken a dose of Benzedrine, that I got my first conviction. I was by now a fully-fledged Teddy Boy (the cult delinquent pose of the 1950s) and as part of my uniform I had got hold of a weapon in the shape of a file, which by its constant jangling in my pocket made me feel that I had really arrived. I was in the company of two ex-Approved School boys who for some bizarre reason decided to visit their old 'home'. I went along simply because I was with them. On the way back a policeman stopped us and on finding the file arrested me. I was charged with possessing an offensive weapon and later conditionally discharged.

The only adult I ever listened to was my mother

but she had no influence over me. At school I could impress my classmates with news about my taboo new world and give first-hand descriptions of the feel of the female anatomy. I was once again a figure of awe and prestige, which only increased my commitment to my new way of life. When I look back on it now, it seems as if I had caught some insidious lowlife disease.

I was on the edge of where the shady, black market culture meets the criminal one and it was obvious that I was going to cross over it. I suppose I might not have turned to crime if these subcultures had not been so accessible or available. Instead I might well have worked out my social and psychological problems without becoming fully infected. The point is these subcultures were there and I chose, and wanted, to enter them.

When I was nearly sixteen I switched from merely rejecting conventional values into positively embracing a criminal morality, which made schoolboy revolt and rebellion otiose. Up to then I had been mixing with youths who straddled the dividing line between legality and illegality in their pursuit of money, though their attitudes were basically anti-social. The police were identified as the enemy; you settled your own disputes with your fists and any weapon you were ruthless enough to use; if you got hurt, you took no action unless it was to make a come-back; if you could turn a dishonest pound, you didn't hesitate to do it.

But such people are not full-time or committed criminals. Dishonesty as an everyday option is a lot different from living by crime. The organised criminal leads a difficult and hazardous life, which only the foolish and optimistic or the patient and cunning believe they can survive.

From my bottom rung of the ladder in this world, I

looked up in adulation to the thieves and tough guys who carried their beliefs to their logical conclusion with all the courage of their convictions. These were men who didn't work and didn't want to work – they lived by crime. At the top of this milieu was a hierarchy of robbers, gangsters, cat burglars and fraudsters who made a success out of crime. This was now the world I wanted to join.

Through my snooker hall contacts, I managed to ingratiate myself into the company of a group of ex-prisoners who were all about nineteen to twenty years old. By the time I was 16, I was a full-time member. With this pool of thieves as a base, I launched out into raiding shops and warehouses or anything else that came along. It started during the summer of 1956. I did not make a fortune, only enough to finance the status symbols of my new life: clothes, parties, girls, even a share in a van. But crime made life a struggle for survival, made it dangerous, dramatic, illegal, demanding, and always exhilarating. I loved it. I don't pretend otherwise.

I threw myself into these ventures with all the zest of a new convert eager to win his spurs. It was like a rite de passage. I stepped voluntarily into the group but, once there, it was like the social processes that occur during indoctrination. What made it easy for me to want to enter this group was my old playground machismo, rejection of authority and not least the lure of some easy money. Moreover, when I was a made member, it was like being in a secret society, where we took risks, relied on each other, were together much of the time and constantly celebrating the same values of staunchness, loyalty, courage and never informing. It was exciting, flamboyant, flattering and had all the camaraderie of a team sport and some.

There was no one in my family with sufficient influence to deflect me from my chosen path. My mother was merely a horrified looker-on; my fathe, in his cups, was already predicting the gallows.

I had entered grammar school with a fairly common set of anti-social values, which sprang from my embryonic macho personality, but they were operating within conventions. Since these conventions were not criminal neither was I, even though my attitudes were potentially criminal. This playground machismo obviously had criminal potential but realising it needed the right conditions or milieu.

Grammar school conventions, however, moderated my machismo and it is possible that even the ethos of learning and work rubbed off on me a little. Although it is noteworthy that it was the bewilderment and hurt to my self-esteem caused by my first examination results that spurred me on to the only real academic effort I ever made – not the desire to acquire the approval of adults or schoolmates.

The disturbances and difficulties of puberty created problems to which my easy access to the criminal subculture provided an answer. Eager to join up, I pulled out my store of anti-social values as my membership card. Once I was accepted I did everything I could to promote my membership. Although I was younger and more innocent than my first criminal companions, I certainly wasn't led astray, recruited, or corrupted by them. It was the attraction of their values and way of life plus the availability of their circle, rather than any induction into crime, that was the determining factor in my adoption of the criminal code.

The professional prisoner

In the summer of 1956 I also took my O-levels. The questions I answered were simply a means of whiling away the time during the examinations. It was a horrible waste and, while I was beyond influencing, I wasn't beyond shame. I felt desolate during these examinations, which no amount of rationalisation could remedy. The previous Christmas I had been entered early for the mathematics exam by a small apoplectic Scot who had inspired a taste for figures in me. He had coached me throughout my schooldays; I worked for that exam and passed it. But it was my only O-level pass. I found compensation for my shame in the derring-do and plunder of a crime.

It didn't last long. In December 1956 four of us were arrested for a whole series of offences, mostly involving shop-breaking, larceny and taking away and driving cars. We were all remanded in custody, but at sixteen I was considered too young for prison and was sent to a remand home in Essex. I was taken there after the court hearing by two big uniformed policemen who delivered me from the back of a dog handler's van and treated me in transit as befitted my surroundings. They made it quite clear that they thought I deserved a good hiding even more than or, preferably as well as, any punishment the court might eventually impose. But I had already decided that I was not going to be treated as a child and that I would escape and join my mates in a real prison.

On delivery at the remand home I was greeted with

rather more respect than most of the inmates, the majority of whom were younger than me – some of them as young as nine or ten. The first thing I felt about my situation was humiliation; I was being treated like a juvenile delinquent and this was something I would not accept. I preferred the dog-van treatment.

All the other children found my presence and my shop-breaking offences heady stuff. I was quickly established as *the man.* I can recall eating my evening meal while small boys vied with each other to eat my cabbage, which as it had to be eaten had become by definition uneatable.

With younger boys hero-worshipping me and my contemporaries submissive, I am rather glad I did not want to stay. Some of the children would be sad cases for the rest of their life. I was only there a few days but I had enough compassion to feel sorry for them.

The principal was a tall, white-haired, tired-looking man, kind but perhaps weary of all the insuperable problems he carried. One evening there was an indoor cricket match on a matt wicket and I delighted in demonstrating my prowess. The principal expressed surprise that anyone who played cricket so well could possibly be a thief. I challenged him to a game of chess and, when he refused, he looked at me for the first time as a child. The next day I ran away.

When I got back to London I rang up my mother and let her persuade me to give myself up. As I had only escaped to be sent to prison with my pals, it was not much of a sacrifice. Considering that this was 1957, it is remarkable how little imprisonment has changed in the intervening years. I loathed it as much then as I do now. Imprisonment has brought me more misery and desperate unhappiness than anything else in my life but not cracking under it is also part of the real criminal's make-up. 'Don't commit the crime, if you can't serve the time' is an adage that is an integral part of the criminal code.

Organised, professional criminals are mindful of what they are doing but outsiders invariably misunderstand the subculture that ideologically underpins what they do. Of course, onlookers are generally only interested in condemning criminals and, as much as they want to understand them, it is with a view to reforming or stopping them. But criminals like me, who are incorrigible and seemingly impossible to deter, are not freaks of nature.

The process by which I became a criminal is perfectly normal. When I entered my first criminal gang, I voluntarily went through a rite of passage that subjected me to a kind of informal indoctrination. Going out with and committing crimes with this group meant that I was constantly soaking up the rules of the criminal subculture. And the latter has certain rules that shaped my identity.

For example, criminals involved in crimes that require a joint enterprise face certain conditions of success. What they are doing is risky and illegal. The risks skyrocket, however, if on arrest any party to the crime follows his own interest and cuts a deal to inform on the others. Criminals do not have to draw up an agreement not to inform because the subculture makes that an inviolate rule. In practice, this means that on a day-to-day basis criminals condition each not to inform and to regard the informer as the lowest form of life. A corollary of this prohibition on informing is that anyone arrested must be prepared to face the music on his own. Criminals also condition each other on this, too. Thus, however much I loathed imprisonment, my self-esteem was based upon it not breaking me. I was honour-bound not to crack, to stay "staunch" as a criminal might put it.

Another example of the way the subculture arms a criminal is in the emphasis it puts on reducing the risks of committing crime. Criminals like myself do not commit crimes if we think there is a strong chance of being caught and punished. To some extent we are only caught and punished if we make mistakes or the police outwit us, although usually that means breaking the law themselves. However, our culture conditions us only to offend when we think we will get away with it. Thus, we cannot be deterred by imprisonment. What risks there are is also romanticised by the subculture. Criminals like myself value risk-taking and derring-do. In the vocabulary, being "game" is a prized virtue. Once you stake your self-esteem on living with the dangers of risk-taking, then being caught is not unlike the chances of getting gored to the bullfighter or of crashing to a racing driver.

Imprisonment is part of the game and this is vividly illustrated by my own reaction to my first dose of it. By the time we were sentenced – two months after arrest – I was already acclimatised to being locked up. I was sentenced to Borstal Training and my three co-defendants, having already completed a Borstal course, were given exemplary sentences of five years. Doubtless the judge saw nothing ironical in the sentence he awarded me.

Nonetheless, I served my time according to the dictates of my criminal culture. Warders – *screws* – were the enemy; you met any insults – anyone taking "liberties" – from other convicts with violence; informers were no different inside than they were outside; sex offenders were an even lower form of life than *grasses*. I hated my jailers and my fellow convicts represented a new arena in which I was driven to struggle for status by living up to the criminal code.

I quickly realised that the prison ran on tobacco and I was soon in business lending out roll-ups at interest rates that would have shamed a loan-shark. I got my first taste of *chokey* for this; I remember being on bread and water for my seventeenth birthday.

The real bottom line of prison is that the hard core inmates interact with each other in accordance with the same criminal code that empowered the commission of their crimes in the first place. With no rational outlet available, such as thieving or gangsterism, this finds expression largely in the cult of toughness for its own sake. This is not to say that modified forms of thieving or gangsterism do not operate. They do, but they are attenuated by the high level of surveillance. Even the cult of toughness is for the most part played out verbally; it is incredible what an amount of repetitive self-enhancing anecdotes pass for conversation in prison.

After another three months at Wormwood Scrubs I was transferred to Portland, a closed Borstal, which was simply a prison by another name. At Wormwood Scrubs there was only one difference between being in Borstal and being imprisoned: Borstal prisoners were given a boiled egg on Friday night. At Portland the only difference lay in the increased facilities for sport, but these were paid for dearly by severer discipline. Sport offers some kind of outlet for machismo and, during my stay at Portland, my life revolved around it.

The prisoners were implacably hostile to the staff and I found myself ideally equipped to share in their beliefs and behaviour. The upshot was our own anti-social values were reinforced in a very direct and uncomplicated way. Not that the screws minded – it was good for their business.

After I had served nineteen months my father died. I was more gratified to receive a few days of home leave than I was disturbed by any grief. I grew up and lived with my father for sixteen years, yet I did not know him. When he died I felt nothing. But ten years later I was involved in bringing up my own son and perhaps for the first time since my father died I thought about him. He was an alcoholic but he always worked incredibly hard. As a child I did not realise this; it was simply that he was constantly in the shop. I subscribe to the belief that the alcoholic drinks in order to retain some semblance of normality; when he was drunk, he simply functioned a little more sluggishly and deliberately. On a few occasions he became incapable of serving in the shop and my mother had to take over, but this rarely happened; mostly he soldiered on with the stock fluctuating according to how hard he was hitting the bottle. Periodically there were money crises and my mother would bail him out after raising a loan from a friend. The accepted treatment for alcoholism in those days was to disapprove of it. My father rotted his insides out and wasted away in hospital at the age of fifty-three.

I remember my callousness now with disgust. What I like to recall is seeing him in the crowd watching me box and, if there is anything in my life I wish he could have seen, it would be me with his grandson. It might have given him a memory that eased his death. My relationship with my own son was entirely different from his with me, but this does not compensate for the way I behaved when he died. I had given my father nothing, not even a little regret at his death.

A month later I was discharged from prison, which actually meant my sentence was discounted by two months. When I came home it was to the shock of a badly neglected business. My mother and sister, who had visited me in prison, had kept back that his little corner shop was close to bankruptcy. I took over the shop, which made me appreciate how hard my father had worked. For a time I immersed myself in it completely and after about a fortnight I had it running smoothly. I suppose this was some tribute to how little imprisonment had handicapped me and it was a worthy achievement for an 18-year-old who had just come out of the nick.

However, my criminality had hardened in prison. No prison in the country is or was as harsh as the conditions in the punishment block at Portland. It was a brutal place, which gave me a fear of imprisonment, but paradoxically also made me contemptuous of it.

That each new indignity
Defeats only the body,
Pampering the spirit
With obscure proud merit.

While my mind was focused on making the family business solvent, my heart was still in crime. I had learned to hate the penal system with a passion and on top of my pretty virulent criminality I now wanted to gain my revenge for the injustices of Portland. Crime is so short and imprisonment so long; it's a rare prisoner who believes that he deserves to be there. I felt hard done by, which I would have felt even if the regime at Portland hadn't been nearly as criminal as I was. Aside from the *get back* syndrome, there is also the *catch up* one. Like a lot of criminals, I had sustained myself in prison with fantasies about how I would make up for it with the good times when I got out. There wasn't much of that working from six in the morning till seven at night.

The critical stage was reached when the shop was solvent – gradually I began to indulge my own desires for a good time with the profits. After I had been out three months, I bought on hire purchase a big flash American car. A Pontiac that cost as much to run as the repayments. I began going out night-clubbing and chasing women, which meant that I could not put in the necessary hours in the shop. When my mother or my sister reproached me, I insulted and abused them with my *right* to make up for those 19 months in prison.

In the course of my pleasure-hunting jaunts, I inevitably made contact with the network of thieves that I knew before I went to prison. I was still not breaking the law but it was only a matter of time. Then I smashed up the Pontiac, which was a pointer to my surfacing recklessness. I also started getting into fights. As a replacement for the Pontiac, I managed to acquire a Ford Zephyr. This faced me with the choices of reducing my spending, plundering the stock and the profits or thieving.

The monotony of life in the shop, the dissatisfactions of my personal life and my turbulent socialising were the conditions in which I chose crime. Psychologically I was still a card-carrying criminal, so my easiest source of self-esteem was enshrining the values of the criminal world. I started shop-breaking. Initially I had some success, but gradually everything fell to pieces and, after I had been out about five months, I brought things to a head by smashing up the Ford Zephyr. My criminal career looked very bleak indeed but my only reaction was to chase my losses by doubling my stakes. This is what criminals do – when their back is to the wall, they take risks.

I spent more and more time out of the shop chasing criminal success. At home there was nothing except constant recrimination, but I was emotionally hooked on a criminal way of life. I came under the influence of a con-man about five years older than myself.

Ray Turner has been the only criminal who ever used me. He eventually turned informer but apart from his unscrupulousness he was extremely charming and manipulative. In a very real way, I came under his spell. He arranged for me and an accomplice to rob a fence, which we duly did, relieving him of a couple of hundred pounds. I held the fence down, while my accomplice took his bank roll. It was a petty run-of-the-mill offence that had been floated by Ray as one that would not be reported. Unfortunately, the fence reported it with a vengeance and my accomplice and I were arrested.

I was remanded in custody. As a result my sister and mother had to take over the shop, which overtaxed their capacity to cope. We had a fairly substantial newspaper delivery service that, as every newsagent knows and no customer does, can lapse into chaos overnight. They had to sell the shop. It wasn't until about six years later that I learned of another fall-out from my arrest. Unable to cope with the situation, my sister turned to the doctor for "help". She was prescribed barbiturates and amphetamines, which led to her becoming a prescription pill addict.

While all this was happening, I was comfortably ensconced in my cell with a good supply of paperbacks. A couple of months later I was tried and found guilty, after a vain effort to secure acquittal. But nightmare of nightmares, I was given another term of Borstal training. My co-defendant, who was twenty-eight years old, was given eighteen months, which meant he would serve twelve with remission. Whereas I was going to be in Borstal for 18 months or more. Of course, the reason for that was I needed training, whereas he was being punished.

Now I had another rationalisation for crime – the unfairness of the criminal justice system. There was also the fact that Borstal was a despised form of punishment in the penal system. Young prisoners, who had been sentenced to a fixed term of imprisonment, were accorded far more dignity by prison warders than "Borstal Boys". Another advantage of imprisonment was that one had an EDR – "earliest date of release".

Borstal Training was an indeterminate sentence of 9 months to 3 years, so one's release was determined by reports and assessments of staff. Thus, the nature of the sentence gave warders far more power over how long one served. The supreme irony of these places was that some were much harsher than prisons. As for "training" – the only training I ever received from prison staff was "a good kicking" when I stepped out of line.

I decided to escape, commit more offences and secure a prison sentence to supplant the Borstal training. By stretching my very limited acting talent to the limit, I managed to induce the assessment officers to send me to an open Borstal. I got what I wanted and was sent to some kind of army camp in the Midlands. I was only there a couple of days, but once I had learned the lay of the land I absconded, taking three others with me.

When I arrived in London I quickly committed a few new offences in case I was suddenly arrested. I wanted to have enough crimes to my name to make sure that I was sent to prison and relieved of my Borstal sentence. This was not unusual and naturally, in exchange for a guilty plea, the police were only too pleased to co-operate with a few judicious words in the witness box about the unsuitability of Borstal for such mature young men. For about three months I was a one-man crime wave: I committed every known crime against property by every known method.

When I was re-arrested, I was sentenced to a fifteen-month prison sentence. Few people have gone more happily to prison. The trouble was the penal system decided to return me to Borstal after I had finished my prison sentence. The worst part of this was the humiliation of Borstal. My sense of injustice took on absurd and obsessive proportions and I was consumed with hatred for the system.

After I finished my prison sentence, I was transferred to the punishment Borstal at Reading. Reading was just a sick prison that catered for sick screws who needed to get off on beating up teenagers. Among its many amenities was a belting on reception and the promise of "a fucking good hiding if you so much as look as if you are going to step out of line". At Reading you did everything at the double, except talk because you weren't allowed to talk. Most of all you did what you were told. And that is about all you did do: what you were told. The only decent thing about Reading was it didn't pretend to *train* anyone in anything except obedience to orders. Eventually the place was closed down after an inquiry instigated by a local MP who exposed the systematic brutality of its regime. No warders were ever charged or disciplined.

I served seven months there and my only thought on release was how quickly and with whom I could get back "at it". I spent my 21st birthday in Reading and I had now served four years in prisons, often under regimes that were supposed to reform or rehabilitate me. I did not know then that this aim is the mythical holy grail of all penal systems in the West and that the only people who benefit from such regimes are the people paid to run them. Nonetheless, while I could not be made law-abiding, it was hardly necessary to actually make me more criminal. Yet, this is what occurred

While I was in prison, my mother and sister had bought a house in Ilford from the proceeds of the sale of the shop. During the six months that I was free, I lived there but I lived off crime. Wage snatch robbery was the trendy crime of the early 1960s and I joined the fashion. During that period my sister gave birth to the first of her two children – both girls. My attitudes and behaviour were indelibly criminal, after six months I was arrested and convicted of riotous assembly and assault. The offence rose out of a restaurant brawl.

The victim started a fight with one of my mates but when it went against him he grabbed a knife from the kitchen. He counter-attacked but was disarmed, then stabbed with his own weapon. He nearly died. I was sentenced to three years. I was also "verballed" for the first time. This is fabrication by the police of incriminating oral admissions. My incriminating admissions provided the basis for confirming my conviction under a *Proviso* ruling at a subsequent appeal. This device allows the Court of Appeal to uphold the verdict even though the trial judge misdirected the jury or, as was the case with me, misinterpreted the rules of evidence. It is done when the Court of Appeal views the trial judge's errors as not significant enough to have affected the verdict of the jury.

I served about two and a half years in Wandsworth Prison. Known to convicts and criminals as the "Hate Factory", Wandsworth had no facilities or amenities. Its main function as its nickname suggests was to the fill convicts with as much hate as possible to ensure that on release they re-offended as quickly as possible. Wandsworth was run strictly for the benefit of prison staff. The monthly visits were closed and lasted 20 minutes; there was no association; no education classes; no TV; no sport of any kind. I worked about sixteen hours a week on the sort of treadmill tasks that prisons specialise in and I had one hour a day walking round the exercise yard. The rest of the time was spent in my cell reading. But I had a *date* (date of release), which is the most important thing in a prisoner's life.

I became a bit of a wheeler dealer in Wandsworth. I ran a betting book, dealt in smuggled goods, trafficked in illicit radio sets. I hustled my way through my sentence. If I had to be inside, Wandsworth offered me everything I needed to confirm my criminality: a regime and a prison staff that provided a justification for my hatred of authority; plenty of illicit rackets to keep my criminal hand in; a load of London gangsters and robbers to mix with; plenty of time in my cell where I could keep fit both physically and mentally.

My attitudes became fixed and stable in Wandsworth. I came out resolved to do better at crime. I was discharged in February 1964. I was still only twenty-three. I changed into my civilian clothes and signed for my property, which included a set of employment cards. I ripped these up and scattered the pieces in the prison corridor. Then I walked out into a world of women, children, colours, scents, traffic, parks – all the things that don't exist in prison.

While I was in Wandsworth my family had sold the house in Ilford and bought another, rather picturesque, cottage-style one in Neasden. Throughout all my time in prison I maintained my links with my mother and sister. My sister, in particular, always visited me and wrote to me in prison, paid for newspapers and books; as well as met crooked warders to help my illicit trading. When I came out of Wandsworth I had no insight into the way she was drowning in the turbulent wake of my mindless cycle of crime and imprisonment. I knew nothing of her pill habit or how unstable she had become.

On my first night out, I did the rounds with some pals I had made in prison and we ended the evening in a night club called *The Jack of Clubs*. I am not a heavy drinker but this night I got drunk, then picked a fight with two fellows over a woman. It was a full-house brawl and more or less exactly the same thing as I had just served a three-year sentence for. Within a week I was looking round for some *work* – someone stuck up a garage payroll. With my new friends I was at it exactly a fortnight after leaving prison.

We steamed into the cash office but, while I was engaged in scooping up the wage packets, my accomplices found themselves facing rather more opposition than they could contend with and deserted me. Unfortunately, they dropped their coshes as they went, which their pursuers gratefully armed themselves with and employed in overcoming me. It was a bracing experience to be on the end of what I normally dished out. Every time I was on the verge of lapsing into unconsciousness, I would give in and, like the good sportsmen, they would allow me to recover and resume hostilities. Eventually, after hearing a judge sentence me to ten years a hundred times, I escaped by diving through a window.

I managed to get far away enough to go to ground like the terrified, bleeding rabbit that I was. During the full-scale man-hunt that followed – which just kept missing me – I nearly had a nervous break-down. For most of the day that the search went on, in my mind I was already in Wandsworth serving a ten-year stretch. My training at lying doggo beat the hunt and I escaped to rob another day.

My sister had spent the day sitting by the radio and, while I did not appreciate it at the time, she went through a hell that wrecked her. She took it a lot harder than I did and was less relieved by the happy ending. The next day, after the euphoria and the post-mortem were over, she cornered me. Her voice was dull and strained and her eyelashes were sticky with tears. She said, "John, please don't do it any more. I couldn't stand it if you went away again. We've everything we need. Harry (a successful business friend) will help you. You can earn good money with him. Please, you're all I've got." It was a plea from a sisterly heart.

By then, I had been in prison for six years and during that time she had done everything for me, including collecting me from the human farms when they let me out. She was trapped in a dull mercenary affair which had wasted her youth and landed her with what was in effect a fatherless child. She was a drug addict and the only person she believed in or was close to was doing his level best to get a really long term of imprisonment. I can remember my reply to her plea, "Don't worry, Jan. Everything will be alright. I'll be careful. Stop worrying."

"I'll be careful." Even then, I was not shifting in my attitude towards crime. My hatred of prison and, more important, my fear of it were as strong a deterrent as there could be. If that day they had passed a law that every convicted robber would be tortured to death, I would later have died under torture. The previous day I had risked a long term of imprisonment after only being out of prison for two weeks. The subsequent manhunt had reduced me to a state of abject terror. By the kind of luck that wins the pools I had got away; no man could ever have been given a better chance and a luckier reprieve. I had strong family ties desperately pulling me away from crime. I was intelligent, quiet and friendly, in many ways the opposite of what the general public assume someone like me is. I had no financial worries and, without much effort, I could have earned a legitimate living. When prison authorities and after-care agencies talk of providing a released prisoner with a home, a job and a supportive background they never even aspire to what I had gratis.

Yet the only effect all these influences had on me was to make me resolve to play a tighter game of robbery than before – to be more careful.

I am labouring in this summary of my situation at 24 years old because its general form is not uncommon among professional criminals. Whatever precipitates the choice of a criminal career – poverty, misery, inadequacy, excitement, greed, malevolence or whatever – once that person becomes immersed in a criminal subculture and his identity locks onto what that subculture celebrates, it is virtually impossible for any outside agency to change him.

I have argued that about the only way to do this is to brainwash the person using the techniques pioneered by the Chinese in North Korea with captured American soldiers. Similar techniques are used by sects like Scientology and hard-line drug therapies such as AA with its Minnesota system. Even where people choose to undergo this kind of psychological engineering there are obvious objections to funding and implementing such schemes.

Nonetheless, while society can't do anything to change people like me when we are in prison, it is in everyone's interest not to licence these establishments to make us worse. It is a cliché to say that while prisons cannot make people better, they can still make them worse and I am a good example of how they did. Some of the prisons I served time in were not especially cruel but they were malignant. I remember one Deputy Governor from Portland seeing me on the exercise yard at Wormwood Scrubs after I was sentenced to 15 months. He rushed towards me and was virtually beside himself with delight at seeing one of his "old boys" back in the system. The other side of the coin of this malignancy is the hypocrisy, lies and delusions of the rehabilitation/reform movement. The probation officers, the social workers and the counsellors are infiltrating the prison system and the recent introduction of parole will compell prisoners to collude in their nonsense.

Yet, for what it matters, as I and others like me know only too well, the best society can do is to ensure that those who catch, convict and imprison us act according to the law. When officials act fairly, justly and humanely we notice it. OK, it does not change us but it impresses us, makes us think, forces us to acknowledge even if only in our heads that the criminal justice system is at least trying to set us an example. That is, in my view, the best society can do and it should certainly do that first before it tries anything else.

My garage escape was a cautionary experience but it didn't make me question my criminality. In about a fortnight I was *working* again. A few days before I was back at it, my sister took an overdose of barbiturates. I fetched the doctor myself from a nearby hospital. The next day the whole unhappy story came out. The precipitating event had been my father's death. She and my mother had to take over the shop before I was released. Janice had become depressed and the doctor had prescribed amphetamines to get her through the long working day that started so early in the morning. This in turn had led to barbiturates to enable her to sleep. By the time the shop was sold she had become dependent. The combination of overworked, sympathetic doctors and, later, the inevitable recourse to the black market added up to a typical case history.

I didn't understand the nature of addiction and had no insight into my own contribution to it. Just like people do with crime, I came up with simplistic explanations and silly exhortations for her to kick her habit. I took her to her local GP as my contribution to a cure. He wrote her a letter of introduction to a psychiatrist who specialised in her problem but after two visits to him she discontinued treatment. Thereafter she continued on her long slide into disintegration, while I carried on hunting the rewards of banditry. It was now the summer of 1964, and the *bag game* was booming. I got my share of what was going and while I was so doing I had a fling with a woman who originated from the same area as I did. She became pregnant and decided to have the child without my encouragement or interest.

I was at liberty for six months, then I was arrested in 1965 by the Flying Squad after a sprawling fight outside my home. I had just taken part in a robbery and was in possession of money, cosh, and overalls and there was also other incriminating evidence. I was charged with the robbery that this evidence related to: a £1,900 wage snatch from a window-cleaning firm. I was also charged with offences connected with the garage robbery for which I had so luckily avoided arrest just after I was released from prison. I was remanded to Brixton Prison and was faced with the prospect of a sentence of anything from seven to fourteen years – which, looked at from my perspective at that moment, did not seem all that different.

My sister visited and, occasionally, the pregnant girlfriend did too. But my sister began going off the rails: she was taking extravagant doses of pills and acting erratically. My demands did not help but she was the only person I could turn to.

On the charge of robbing the window-cleaning firm, I was indicted with three other defendants who were out on bail. There was the usual manoeuvring going on between solicitors, the Flying Squad and the other defendants. A deal was cut for me to plead guilty to the window-cleaning robbery and not guilty to robbing the garage. After about three months on remand I was tried on the latter charge and acquitted. I never paid the money for the "help" that I was given to dilute the evidence.

As the trial on the remaining charge came nearer, my sister was in a permanent narcotic stupor and she started quarrelling with my mother and and even selling my clothes – things that she would never have done normally. Now everything fell upon my mother: she was bowed down by money troubles and, with my sister cracking up, everything became too much for her. I quarrelled with my sister about her behaviour but she did something she had never done before – she simply insulted me, told me I could do what I liked and left me to it.

For once, the sheer misery of their existence and my responsibility for it, took its toll on me. The enormity of what I had inflicted on my family broke through the protective ideological shell of my criminal identity. The scale of my criminal failures was also unavoidable. Then hovering in the background was the pregnant girlfriend. I decided to plead not guilty to the window-cleaning robbery, although the evidence against me was virtually watertight. The deal I struck with myself was to go for a not guilty and, if I got a result, then pack up crime. I like to think now that I would have honoured my commitment.

Certainly, the crisis in my sister's life and my mother's despair shamed me. Although I did not recognise my full responsibility in causing them, I recognised that it was my duty to deal with them. The basic character of my values and beliefs remained unchanged but the distress of my mother and sister plus my failures as a criminal had got through to me. I was also coming to terms with the fact that I was too impatient, too careless and, perhaps, too indifferent to material gain to succeed as a criminal.

Before my arrest I had started to meet and associate with a number of people whose efforts in business had brought them far greater success than my criminal ventures. The writing of my criminal failure was on the wall and while I could not understand how I had converted to crime I could read that it was time to do something different.

There were secondary considerations in my decision to plead not guilty, mostly connected with the nature of the evidence against me. There was an abundance of damning evidence but the Yard had over-egged it. They had also produced enough *verbals* (fabricated oral incriminating admissions) to make a long-playing record; plus also some evidence, based on false observation, which tended to incriminate my co-defendants by association with my own obvious guilt. My co-defendants had protested all along against my agreement to plead guilty, though I can't say they put any real pressure on me to change my plea.

What really confirmed me in my decision to renege on my deal with the Yard was the way I could turn the evidence of the concocted verbal admission on its head. I knew that if I defended myself and the jury was exposed to me constantly over a two week trial rather than just a guest appearance in the witness box they would never believe that I had said these verbal admissions. In those days, *verbal* was done without much thought and even the words attributed to me were contrary to my pattern of speech. My defence was: "If the police are lying, you members of the jury have no choice other than to acquit."

At the first trial, before Sir Carl Aarvold, the jury acquitted one of us and hung on eleven to one in favour of acquitting the others including me. At a retrial in front of Judge Rogers, the jury, after deliberating for seven hours, acquitted one defendant and convicted two of us, Roy Nash and me. He was sentenced to five years to run concurrently with a two-year sentence he had just begun. I was sentenced to eight years. The bench did not approve of my decision to defend myself.

I gambled and I lost. Yet, I also worked my socks off intellectually for the first time since my first year at Grammar School. Of course, the Yard were furious. As they thought I was going to plead guilty, they hadn't taken much care with the evidence against me. This gave me the opportunity to run riot with their contradictions and lies. They finally got a result but some of them were humiliated in the witness box. After the second trial, one of these detectives said to the acquitted Danny Shay, "McVicar's in the frame, and he'll never come out of it."

I went back to Wandsworth, but within four months I was in Parkhurst. I was now twenty-five. Eight years is a long time when you are already punch-drunk with imprisonment. For the first time in my life I felt cut off from the world. I rarely had any letters or visits and my break with my sister hurt. My mother, as usual, was still sweeping up the wreckage, but by now despair had ingrained itself into her mind and I could not listen to her without feeling the guilt of my irresponsibility. I retreated into myself.

I had become disillusioned with crime and with my criminal identity, but there was nothing else. I belonged to the world I was in and had no other one to turn to. I went through the motions of serving my time but I ducked out of the prison power play. I did a bit of sport – Parkhurst left us to our own devices – but otherwise I was an ex-player, retired but basically unchanged.

Then an opportunity to escape presented itself. Prisoners are always feuding and there was a stabbing in our wing that one of the suspected parties used in the ensuing police investigation to get a break from prison routine by going to court. He partially faked his own guilt with the investigating detectives in order to have charges preferred against him, which meant standing trial at Winchester Assizes. It was a joke that turned serious.

A number of other cons who saw the possibility of escaping badgered him to call us as witnesses. The accused trial was a shambles and he was found guilty, sentenced to five years even though he was innocent. On the way back to Parkhurst from Winchester Assizes court, nine of us escaped from the prison coach. Two of us got away – I was one of them.

I was at large from the end of May to the middle of September 1966. I went back at it but without much purpose other than getting enough money to get by. But I was certainly active. I was re-arrested after an aborted robbery but then I was charged with firing on a police car in Deptford. I drew another 15 years for this "making 23 years in all" as Mr Justice Hinchliffe lovingly intoned. The arresting charge got me 5 years consecutive. I relapsed again into criminal rationalisations: since detectives flouted the laws of evidence as flagrantly as I robbed, then I was justified in being a criminal. It was intellectually pathetic but who wants to feel guilty on top of serving 23 years?

I have to say again, however, that even when their back is to the wall people like me are not blind. Judge Maude, who dealt with the aborted robbery charge, was decent and just. It wasn't merely that he showed me mercy in not adding to my sentence but in the manner he treated me. Without making a song or dance of it, he acknowledged the mess that I had made of my life and didn't compound it. Even though it didn't matter to me what my sentence was I thanked him in open court for his clemency.

The last crime

I had spent a year on solitary at Wandsworth, but after the aborted robbery trial I was moved immediately to Chelmsford Prison. I was involved in a failed escape attempt, then moved to Durham Prison. On 26th October 1968 I escaped, reaching London three days later. Some time later, I went back to the woman who bore my child. Everything was shadowed by my 23-year sentence, which now hung over my illegal liberty like a sword of Damocles. Any small mistake or stroke of fate would put me back in prison for minimum of 15 years. But that did not prevent me from involving myself in my son's life.

Russell was four when I escaped and in early February of the following year he was sitting on the floor talking to a friend when I suddenly saw in him myself as a child. It was like a flashback in a movie and instead of him I suddenly saw myself as I was at his age. It was extremely vivid even down to the clothes that I wore as a child. Until then I had simply accepted him as my son but not with any emotional depth. It shook me as I was immediately aware of the symbolism of what my imagination had done.

I rushed into the kitchen to tell his mother but more about the emotional impact of the incident than its symbolism. She did not understand my excitement because as his mother she had always felt the bond of identification that attaches a child to his or her parents. The experience did not change the way I treated my son but it had a powerful impact on my feelings for him; in turn it had a powerful impact on the way I felt about myself. The side effects of my criminal antics had already damaged my own family, now I was exposing my son to the same heartache and danger.

At that age, Russell did not know that I was his father since his mother had always felt that, as I could not be a proper father, it was best he did not know. I was "Uncle Tommy". However, a few months later we did tell him and it had a powerful impact on him – every bit as strong as the effect my flashback experience had had on me. He told his mother in one terribly poignant revelation that he knew other children had dads but he didn't think he did. "Dad" became his favourite word. When he was playing with his toys, he would sit chanting it like a mantra.

He idolised me and I was acutely aware that if I was re-arrested not only would he miss me terribly but also would damage him emotionally. All he wanted was to be around me and do what I did. As I was mostly at home, we had a lot of time together and I taught him the rudiments of chess and how to read. He was desperate to please me and to be like me.

While I was inordinately grateful to have opened up a window of life that hitherto I had not known, I was acutely aware of the implications of it for his long-term development. All the guilt and agonising over this made me do something I should have done years before: it made me examine myself and the life I was leading. I had squandered nearly all my youth and hocked much of my future in an utterly irresponsible, reckless criminal career that only by luck, not judgement, had not left anyone dead or crippled, but it had wasted grotesque amounts of public money. I had inflicted permanent damage on my own mother and sister, then I had escaped against all the odds to an existence that could only be funded by crime. Yet, as a sideshow, I was now playing father with my son in circumstances that were impossible to sustain. At some stage, I was going to deprive him of his father just as I had been deprived of mine.

I had the same surge of energy then as when I defended myself in a last-ditch attempt to avoid imprisonment. There was also the same disillusionment with my criminal career that I had felt at that time. I began thinking and reading. Bertrand Russell once noted, "Many people would rather die than think. In fact they do." I decided I wasn't going to be one of them.

I knew that my own relationship with my son could never be anything like that between my father and me; but I started thinking about my father for the first time since he died. I started to read books on child psychology – I suppose to try to understand the development of my own son – but it quickly grew into a passion to try to analyse and understand my own childhood.

My effort left me with some insight into my upbringing, but not any understanding of how and why my criminality had emerged and developed. In particular, I was mystified as to why I had obdurately and incorrigibly persisted in crime despite spending far more time in prison than I had outside. I had been a disaster to myself but I had proved incapable of understanding it and changing my life accordingly. In a very real way, I did not make sense to myself.

I remembered my prison dossier, which I had read and destroyed during a riot in Durham prison before I escaped. It was a massive document consisting of thousands of reports assembled on me over all the years I had been in prison. I had gone through it methodically hoping to unlock the key on what was already a puzzle to me – why I had compulsively continued to be a criminal. It contained nothing of interest. The people who had controlled my life for years and years knew far less about me in a criminological sense than I did myself. And I certainly didn't know much. I was actually more shocked than disappointed that so much money and time had been spent on compiling this worthless mountain of paper. The memory of this con on the taxpayer now became part of my motivation to do the job that these people had pretended to do.

I read a lot about ideology, role theory and some text books on criminology. I was hardly a unique or difficult subject to understand and I certainly gained for myself a reasonable insight into my development. I have tried to convey that understanding in this peculiar defence document. Of course, we all know more than we can articulate, and I am conscious that I haven't conveyed the analysis that well. I have only a smattering of psychology, criminology and sociology to work with, but whatever the flaws of this peculiar defence document it remains true to me. It describes what was a genuine advance in self-awareness and its validity is that this exercise changed me.

The irony is that this change was made in circumstances that were hardly conducive to leading a law-abiding life! I had the choice of giving myself up or attempting to accumulate sufficient funds to finance a life abroad with Russell and his mother. I understood that this was a pipe dream but it was the only shot I had and I went for it. It is a choice that I do not regret. Yet the one thing I did decide was that whatever the outcome – abroad or back to prison – I would never go back to crime. That was inviolate. And I knew that it would be an easy pact to honour because crime no longer claimed me. Crime was now something I did to make money not to validate my identity or test my mettle. One effect of this was that it made me far more cautious and rational, which is why I stayed at large for two years. That period is actually longer than the accumulated periods of freedom I have had since I left school.

Self–evidently I failed in stealing enough money to go abroad. But I admit I tried, which is why I am now charged with possession of an armoury of tools and guns that only had one purpose. My career as a criminal is over. A wag might retort, "Yes, because you're already on 23 years and facing more time." Well, it bears remembering that people like me do not stop being criminals when they go to prison. The way I served time was apiece with the way I committed robberies. I was locked into the same game.

My mother once instinctively summed this up in an extremely insightful comment. I was in the house talking with some of my criminal pals about prison and she observed: "You must all like it in there, you are always in there – and when you're not, you're always talking about it." There is a profound emotional truth to her comment.

Criminals like I was serve their time just like I did. I don't serve my time like a criminal anymore. I don't curry favour with prison staff but I am not disruptive, nor will I try to escape again. I will use my time to study and re-educate myself, to pick up where I left off at Grammar School. That is what I shall do. When I am released I will work, hopefully using the fruits of my prison studies.

On the set of the film *McVicar* with Roger Daltrey who played me, Cheryl Campbell who played Russell's mother and Ricky Parkingson who playedmy son, Russell.

I am not going to pretend that I feel any genuine guilt about the crimes I have committed. I have never killed or maimed anyone and neither have I ever stolen enough money to retire on. I like to think that if I had done the former I would be ashamed of it. My guilt lies in what I did to my family. My mother driven to a shadow of her real self; my sister unable to cope without medication; the mother of my son arrested for harbouring and put in prison; my son now exposed to a fatherless upbringing. My shame overreaches whatever punishment I face.

My arrest was the result of betrayal by a friend. Even that causes me no bitterness. I will not seek revenge, such things have no part to play in what I intend to salvage from my future.

I am only too well aware of Lord Birkett's saying that "to explain human behaviour is not always to excuse it". As I have admitted, I continued to commit criminal acts when my criminality has ceased to have any power over me, which might be said to make me more culpable. I made the choice and I must suffer the consequences. I can sympathise with the objective view that there must be some retribution for these offences. I also know that the only punishment available to the bench is a further increase in my sentence. My current sentence already means that with good behaviour I must serve another 12 years. Of course, I could be paroled but that is unlikely to be in under ten years. By then I will be forty, having spent twenty years in prison. These are the facts.

When I began to serve my present sentence two of my co-defendants were acquitted and the remaining one, Roy Nash, was convicted. Judge Rogers gave me eight years, a sentence I shall finish, if I am a good boy, by April 1974. He sentenced Roy Nash to five years, concurrent with a two-year sentence he had just begun. Nash has been out of prison for nearly three years now, mainly, I suppose, because of his wife and son, who was born about the same time as my own. He has worked hard and never returned to crime. He may not be the straightest man in the world, but he will never relapse into banditry.

I saw him when I was out of prison; he is my friend and I felt happy for him, but I also felt an ineffable sadness at the difference in our circumstances. He escaped from the coach with me on our way back to Parkhurst but he was caught that day while I went on to commit more offences for which I drew another 15 years. Perhaps it is the luck of the draw.

Luck like mercy is not a quality it is wise to rely on. Perhaps freedom is the most precious thing a man possesses, more precious than absence of pain or suffering, and maybe that is why taking it away is the only real means of punishment the bench retains in our civilised times. All the crimes I have committed since I began my eight–year sentence were committed while I was chasing freedom. I don't know if that "excuses" any more than it "explains". In the end, perhaps, all I can do is to hope for some luck and ask for some mercy.

Perhaps, Malcolm Morris, you can pick something out of this statement that will assist you in preparing my defence. I apologise for so complicated and profitless an undertaking.

John McVicar,
July 1971.

(After listening to Malcolm Morris QC and reading this document, the trial judge sentenced McVicar to three extra years, making 26 years in all. He served 11 years and was released in 1978.)

ARTNIK BOOKS
341b Queenstown Rd SW8 4LH
+44 (0) 20 7498 1257
ArtnikBooks@dsl.pipex.com

SALES & DISTRIBUTION

LITTLEHAMPTON Book Services
Faraday Close, Worthing
BN13 3RB UK
DDI: 01903 828860
bmr@lbsltd.co.uk